ADVANCE PR

"The transition from founder-CEO to successor-CEO is a critical inflection point for a startup, and unfortunately is rarely smooth. Les Trachtman was deeply involved with half a dozen of those inflection points and has the scars and hard-learned lessons (and successes) to prove it. Before you head into such a transition, save yourself much pain by learning from Les' insights and the best practices he has developed."

—**NOAM WASSERMAN**, founding director, Founder Central Initiative; professor of clinical entrepreneurship, University of Southern California; best-selling author of *The Founder's Dilemmas: Anticipating and Avoiding the Pitfalls That Can Sink a Startup*

"This book should be a prerequisite for all start-up founders. It's also beneficial for founders who have been running companies for 20 or 30 years and are experiencing stagnant growth. If you're honest with yourself and want your company to achieve the next level, you must read this book. Now!"

—**RICHARD SPANTON**, Jr., founder and chairman, AccuLynx.com

"There is no one more qualified than Les Trachtman to write on the subject of the handoff from the founder to the professional CEO. Les writes from experience, and it is not always pretty. *Don't F**k It Up* is a practical compilation of vignettes written from the trenches that is essential reading for anyone faced with the prospect of taking over from a founder. Beware!"

—**HAROLD FRIED**; professor, Union College; David L. and Beverly B. Yunich Chair of Business Ethics

"We all want to believe that our company is special. The truth, however, is that we face many of the same challenges. This book is a fantastic summary of some of the critical issues that CEOs and founders have struggled through, and outstanding advice on how to best navigate them. I think it's the most valuable read for any new CEO that I have found."

—**ROBERT LANGONE**, CEO, Automated Dynamics

How Founders and Their Successors Can
Avoid the Clichés That Inhibit Growth

DON'T
F**K
IT UP

LES TRACHTMAN

RIVER GROVE
BOOKS

This publication is designed to provide accurate and authoritative information in regard to the subject matter covered. It is sold with the understanding that the publisher and author are not engaged in rendering legal, accounting, or other professional services. If legal advice or other expert assistance is required, the services of a competent professional should be sought.

Published by River Grove Books
Austin, TX
www.rivergrovebooks.com

Copyright ©2017 Leslie S. Trachtman

Distributed by River Grove Books

Design and composition by Greenleaf Book Group
Cover design by Greenleaf Book Group

Cataloging-in-Publication data is available.

Print ISBN: 978-1-63299-129-4

eBook ISBN: 978-1-63299-130-0

First Edition

To my mother, June Trachtman, *who has been an elementary school teacher for almost four decades. She encouraged me, and hundreds of students, to love to learn. She also told me that any idiot could spell. Years later, spell checkers were invented to save me.*

ONE: MESSING WITH SUCCESS   9

"Don't f**k it up."

"I know more about this company than anyone ever will."

"I could have told you that would happen."

"Next time run these things past me."

TWO: SEEKING HIGHER GROUND   27

"We'll never find someone who can do this as well as me."

"It's better if I do this myself."

"Next time I'll let someone else handle it."

"I think you might want to reconsider what you are about to do."

THREE: THEY'RE EXPECTING ME   45

"That customer and I have a long-standing relationship."

"I'll just take this customer's call."   .

"I don't have time to record all this stuff in our system."

"In the grand scheme of things, this won't make any difference."

FOUR: JUST ASK WHY   67

"I'm OK hiring someone as long as they don't slow me down."

"That's how we do it here."

"I'm not sure you understand how different this company is."

"That would mean giving up a key advantage."

ACKNOWLEDGMENTS

This book is a product of several years of starts, stops, procrastination, and then restarts. It finally came to life when I committed to a Kickstarter project during the end of the summer of 2014. There was a host of people who agreed sight unseen to fund its first printing, thereby encouraging me to focus on completing the project.

Several people went above and beyond in their support of this book. These people include Dr. Mark Baganz, cofounder of Purview, a partner, customer, and trusted advisor of mine; Bill Diederich, one of the finest successors a founder could ever hope for; and David Reinhardt, my friend for more than three decades, and the smartest person with whom I ever worked (at least according to him).

Other supporters include Dave Toole, the best CFO I've ever worked with and a trusted friend; Kurt Johnson, a company founder with great insight, wisdom, and a guy I'd gladly work for; Harold Fried, a passionate entrepreneur, teacher, friend, and colleague who gave me the opportunity to learn how to be a good board member and introduced me to my potential successor; and Bruce Johnson, a consummate professional CEO who successfully harnessed a most challenging board of directors. I'd also like to acknowledge Dave Blakelock, who is a fellow alumnus of Union College, and a partner in promoting entrepreneurship at Union—and, as he is fond of noting, the very first backer of this book.

I had the unique pleasure of having Noel Weyrich coach and edit my writing in this book. Despite my stubbornness, Noel was able to get me to consider and reconsider many of my ideas, resulting in a better product. This book would just not have been the same without Noel doing his magic on the jumbled words that I put together and called chapters.

I'm indebted to my wife, Michelle, who has been my partner and supporter through all of my (mis)adventures, and who put up with the weekend warrior writer that I became. My daughter, Megan, has also been one of my biggest supporters and is a quick learner of this crazy thing we call "business." She will no doubt be a founder one day. My son, Rob, was one of my first editors. His exacting style always takes a toll on my ego, but it certainly made this manuscript a better read. He is a student of management, and my hope is that there is some important advice between these covers that will benefit him in his career. David Reinhardt also took on the thankless task of editing an early draft, which he summarily rejected, helping make this a far better manuscript. I'm sure I can never repay him for his guidance, direction, and support of both this book and various portions of my career. But I am certain he will remind me of this and will exact his share of psychic value.

My sincere thanks go out to Noam Wasserman, formerly of the Harvard Business School and now at the Lloyd Greif Center for Entrepreneurial Studies at the University of Southern California, heading up their Founder Central initiative, whose early probing of my successes and failures helped me understand myself as a founder-successor and ensured that my heading would improve in subsequent endeavors. Thanks also to Matt Marx, who picked up the case and included me in some extremely lively discussions in his class when he taught at the Sloan School at MIT. Noam and Matt are critical resources for the next generation of budding entrepreneurs, who will be more prepared than ever for the unique issues surrounding founders and their successors. I am also indebted to Matt for his willingness to add his foreword to my story.

Most of all I am appreciative of the founders, the board members, and the employees of the organizations with whom I have had the privilege to work. I'm especially indebted to Gordon Rapkin, my first and several-times-since boss. He is a successful founder in his own right and a mentor who can translate technology into business as effectively as anyone I've met. My CEO career was perhaps most impacted by Mike Brody, who, despite my initial stumble as a first-time CEO, took a chance and asked me to join his organization. None of the rest of my journey would have happened if Gordon or Mike hadn't had the intuition (or perhaps the guts) to hire me.

Thanks!

FOREWORD

At MIT I teach an entrepreneurship class where we have about a dozen guest speakers during the semester. At the end of the course, I ask students to rank the speakers. Les was their favorite. I hope this foreword helps explain why. First, a digression . . .

A few years ago a "friend" of mine persuaded me to register for a bike race up Mount Washington in New Hampshire. Its peak is 6,288 feet, with an average grade of 12 percent and reaching 20 percent in some places. If you knew me, you'd be scratching your head at this decision, as I'm not exactly one of those cyclists with zero body fat. In fact, I think I hold the record for the slowest time ever up the mountain on two wheels. The only way I was able to make it was to outfit my bike with very low gearing. (For the gearheads, a 24-tooth front chain ring mated to a 36-tooth cog in back—only 18 gear-inches.) This gearing made it possible for me to pedal the seven miles up the mountain.

Starting a company is in some ways like climbing a steep mountain. You're working like crazy, but it feels like you are making very slow progress. Founders have to be able to handle failure and frustration as they struggle to develop their product or service, figure out a business model, and try to attract talent who will probably have a higher expected return at some other company. To some extent, resilient founders are like that very low gear on my bicycle—continuing to pedal even on a very steep grade.

At some point, though, the startup may break through and start to get traction. Things get easier, and concerns shift from mere survival to speeding things up. It's as if the sharp grade of the mountain flattens out and you can accelerate. In fact, there is a spot on Mount Washington, just before the final climb, where the road flattens out for maybe a quarter-mile. To pick up your pace, you need to shift gears. When I reached this spot, that 24–36 gearing configuration that enabled me to get up the 12 percent incline was a liability. I checked once, and the fastest I could go on flat ground with that gearing was 3.5 mph. Maybe a professional cyclist could go 5 mph or maybe 7 or 8, but not 25 or 30. You need to shift into a higher gear to maximize speed.

Now, some founders have the ability to shift from the low gear that gets them through the tricky early stages to a higher gear that enables the company to accelerate and realize its potential. They are household names: Zuckerberg, Dell, Gates, Knight, etc. Their examples are so well known that I worry sometimes we become "success biased" in that we think that's how starting a company always works.

But the data shows otherwise. Multiple academic studies reveal that between one-third and one-half of founding CEOs get replaced, and not just when things go poorly. It is, ironically, exactly once that company has scaled the steepest grades of the mountain and begun to need to accelerate on the flatter portion that the need for a "gear change" becomes apparent (often driven by investors). It can be in both the company's best interest and even the entrepreneur's best interest—at least in the long term—to bring in someone new.

Les is that new someone. He has been the "second CEO" at a half-dozen companies at this point and can speak authoritatively about this transition from early-stage hill climbing to later-stage growth and acceleration. He understands not only the necessity for the change but the art of doing it right: entering the right way (usually as a less threatening consultant), figuring out how to take charge, and helping founders step aside gracefully.

It's a story that isn't told very often. That's why my students picked Les as their favorite speaker. There is too much cheerleading in entrepreneurship education these days, where students are told "everything is awesome" (or will be) as an entrepreneur. That may be, and again, there are a small number of salient success stories where the founders control the company from day one. But for many, if not most startups, a transition will come.

—Matt Marx
Associate Professor, Boston University

Previously, Marx was Associate Professor of Technological Innovation, Entrepreneurship, and Strategic Management and the Mitsui Career Development Professor of Entrepreneurship at the Sloan School of Management, MIT.

INTRODUCTION

I 've wanted to write this book since my fourth experience succeeding a company founder. I was fresh off a somewhat raw departure and trying to reconcile my successes and failures along the way. I was two for four. In baseball, that batting average would put me in the Hall of Fame. But, even with the successes I had, something was still frustrating me.

About this time, Noam Wasserman, a professor at the Harvard Business School who had adopted "founder frustrations" as a focus for his research, contacted me. Noam was teaching a course called Founders' Dilemmas, aimed at helping students understand the opportunities and obstacles of founding companies and working with company founders. He had read one of my blogs and suggested that my recent experiences were a perfect backdrop for a case he was writing about founders' successors. I thought it would be interesting to have my career be the subject of a Harvard Business School case.

As the case took form, an important theme emerged. If a founder was ready for change, then together we could navigate toward great success. But if the founder was not ready to accept change, it didn't matter what advice I provided—it would likely be ignored.

Each time Noam taught the case *Les Is More Times Four*, he invited me to attend. The classes were both challenging and invigorating. I learned more about myself as well as the founders I've worked with in each session. Based upon Noam's course rankings and his repeated invitation over the years, I think students got something out of it as well. The case has now been taught at the Sloan School at MIT, the Smith School at Maryland, and other leading business programs around the world. These classes have taught me that if you have the opportunity to have your life scrutinized by hundreds of really smart business students, you should take full advantage—just be sure you have a thick skin.

I've gone on to two more founder startups since the case was written, a total of six, making me the most experienced founder successor alive! My experience has ranged from taking over the CEO role from a founder in a venture-backed pre-revenue startup to running a $350 million twenty-year-old company when the founder grew tired of his changing industry. Several of the companies I led were sold for several times their gross revenue, making their founders rich.

Like the majority of founder-led ventures, each of my transitions involved the founder sticking around after I took over the CEO role. And while founders staying involved in the ventures past their succession is the general rule, it makes the situation for their successor much more challenging. Together we made the difficult adjustments to grow these companies and increase their value—although we often disagreed on the path. Three out of five ventures experienced wealth-building liquidity events for these founders and their stakeholders. Two I'd have to characterize as failures (although the venture capitalists at both would have you believe otherwise), enabling me to learn some of the most important lessons contained in this book. The sixth is still a work in progress, with a recent valuation of more than six times the value from when I arrived two years prior, inspiring me to think deeply about my succession.

After all of these experiences and the self-awareness that the Harvard case provided, I am eager to share the lessons I have learned with you. I know that every founder believes his company is special, exceedingly complex, and unique. I can assure you that the challenges confronting you are just not that different. Ninety-five percent of your problems are shared by other founders, which is good news because it means your problems are solvable. They've been seen and handled many times before—all that is required is the smarts and the courage to address them.

If you are taking the time to read this book, you have already proven you are eager to learn. So, the key to your future success is *courage*. The most successful founders I encountered realized that despite their success, they didn't actually understand everything that ultimately needed to be done for their organizations. These founders were willing to accept risks that come with growth. They were willing to try new approaches, recruit new people with different backgrounds than themselves, and seize opportunities that risked destroying the work they had previously accomplished. With the courage to break the things that weren't broken, bury their egos, seek help to complement their skills, and upgrade their founding teams, and with the audacity to realize that their ventures were not just all about them, these entrepreneurs would reach the ultimate heights their ventures deserved.

This book's title, *Don't F**k It Up,* was something that was said to me by one of these founders as I took over the reins of his company. His meaning was clear. He wanted me to be sure to not screw up the hard work and success that he had accomplished before my arrival. But that's just the point. To scale your company, you have to be willing to f**k things up.

I believe that every founder will recognize him- or herself in the pages of this book. It is structured as a series of challenges and lessons—each reflective of the clichés that a founder should never say. Some viewpoints will resonate with you. Some you will disagree with. But as you dig into the concepts, you will surely recognize that there is more than just a single right or wrong way to proceed.

You can read the chapters in this book continuously or refer to them separately as the need arises. Each chapter encourages you to test yourself, be introspective, and question whether the view you currently hold is based upon solid reality or instead is a creation of what others around you want you to hear and see. Depending upon the stage of your venture, a particular chapter may be applicable today while another may not yet be relevant. Keep the book around and refer to it from time to time as you continue down your path.

Chapter One encourages empowering others in your organization to participate in some of the important decisions. Founders have a tendency to micromanage and control large domains within their organizations. But in order to scale, you will have to give up that behavior and accept the risk that someone may just f**k something up. You will have to deal with it.

Chapter Two begins with the realization that you can't continue to do everything as your organization grows. You'll begin to give up some of your current responsibilities to make way for a more important focus. Finding people to take over your former roles will be challenging. You will hire executives who may not seem to be as good as you at the tasks you are leaving behind. Sometimes throwing them in the deep end is the best training they can get for this new role, and their results might surprise you. The theme of Chapter Two is building institutional muscle to free you up to do more important tasks.

The third chapter begins your climb up The Founder Value Ladder. Despite all your hard work and dedication to getting your organization going, it is no longer all about you! You shed some tasks in order to take on newer, higher-value opportunities. To set your company up for growth and longevity, you'll need to begin the deflating task of separating your identity from that of your organization. This means weaning your customers and stakeholders off relying on you alone, from negotiating their special deals directly with you to calling you on your cell phone when they need something. Although they may be disappointed at first, it's in their (and your) best interests. But whether or not to climb the ladder is a choice that every founder must make. The heights are not suitable for all. Maximizing your personal goals may mean getting off the ladder early.

Chapter Four challenges you to bring in new resources to fill the gap in your experience. Finding someone who has the capabilities but lacks the direct experience in your business or industry can be just the prescription for your next growth phase—a "beginner," as Steve Jobs would call her. Someone who asks the naïve questions may be just what you need to expose important truths.

Prepare to shed your skin. In Chapter Five, you will sever old friendships and part with family executives. The company has outgrown them. Like the snake that sheds its skin in order to grow, you need to shed some founding executives to make way for a new crop of professionals with different skill sets to lead this leg of your journey. Your new team won't be nearly as deferential, even if you are not ready for that.

In Chapter Six, you'll reach out to others for help. The CEO job is a lonely one. Seek out a resource that can help you cope and who will help you gain perspective. If you are lucky, you will find that you've been running around naked like the emperor who had no clothes. Unfortunately, it's more likely that your current loyal constituents are sugarcoating their results. Instead, you need to find someone who can help you find the unvarnished truth.

It's now getting near the time for you to step back; time for you and your company to plan out separate futures. Chapter Seven provides a road map for preparing both yourself and your organization for the day you step out. Making yourself superfluous even while you are still present will strengthen your organization and give you the flexibility to plan for your afterlife.

When it comes time to step away, you should step out completely. As Chapter Eight describes, the worst thing you can do is stick around and second-guess your successor. Go off and enjoy your new freedom and let your organization head in its own direction. Support your successor completely; be there—but only as her counsel when she requests it—you'll both end up better for it.

If you are a founder, a successor to a founder, an investor in a founder-led organization, an executive working for a founder, or on the board of a founder-run organization, you owe it to yourself and your founder to understand his plight. You will no doubt find founder behaviors you recognize, precepts that have puzzled you, and ideas that you can put to use to improve your organization within this book.

No matter what your role, if your life touches that of a founder, you will find ideas that will resound truthfully. My hope is that *Don't F**k It Up* will enable you to discover shortcuts from the path that I have taken and accelerate your knowledge growth using my experiences.

Running a company as a founder or CEO is a difficult job. Despite how some view it, making hard decisions that affect people's lives and livelihoods cannot be taken lightly. To scale your venture, you must be willing to do the hard things that cause you to lose some friends along the way. As one of my board members once suggested, "If you want a friend, get a dog."

I've had several great dogs over my career.

ONE

MESSING WITH SUCCESS

*"Don't f**k it up!"*

It was the autumn of 2008 and the global economy had cratered.

At the time, I was several quarters into my tenure as the new COO of a company in the government-procurement industry, and my work there had just begun to bear fruit. We'd improved our gross margins and the bottom line was growing. But the credit crisis suddenly put us in a very precarious position, as it did with many other companies that fall. We urgently needed to make some bold moves to accelerate our pace of change. Our borrowing capacity was not sufficient to fund our sales growth. Even with increased sales volume our margins were not sufficient to generate ample enough profits. Our systems and our processes needed an overhaul to handle the larger order volume.

The company's founder was a larger-than-life charismatic leader.

He was happy with the progress we'd been making, and although he understood the need for fast action in the face of crisis, he was also very nervous. Change meant we would be breaking from the script he'd created and followed since the company's beginning. One day when we were wrapping up a conversation about the changes, he ended with a few words of caution.

"OK," he said, "but don't f**k it up."

I didn't pay much heed to his words in that moment, but the strain in his voice—joking and at the same time deadly serious—remains a vivid memory. I had heard the founder utter the phrase casually to others in the company. It was his small way, I assumed, of dealing with his feelings of discomfort when giving up control. My guess is that if you've never said this in a joking way to one of your key employees, you've probably thought it.

Over time, however, I've come to realize that seemingly harmless little comments like "Don't f**k it up," "Get it right," or even "Be careful" are among the worst things you can say to an employee. That's because while you may say it as a joke, your employees will hear it very differently. They hear "Don't fail—or else."

They hear you warning them not to take risks, not to try new things, not to attempt anything that might not work.

Is that what you want your employees' marching orders to be? Not if you want to grow and scale your company. You want them to show initiative and take measured risks that yes, occasionally, might not work. There are always unforeseen challenges involved when you blaze new trails, and the people you've hired need to know in advance that it's OK while trailblazing to hit some dead ends and even fall off a few cliffs.

WHY YOU NEED TO F**K IT UP

The irony is that every founder knows the need for innovation very well. You created new value in the market by doing things others couldn't or wouldn't do, and you suffered plenty of foul-ups and failures along the way. Growing your business requires your employees to advance with that same spirit of adventure and discovery. Teams innovate and grow their abilities when they are free to experiment and then collaborate on solving the new problems exposed by their setbacks and failures. You want to challenge your team to try things that might fail at first. You want them to become adept at recognizing failure quickly, regrouping, and then trying again. But then realize success.

Success is the brass ring for entrepreneurs. It's what you put in all those long hours for. It's how you keep score. It's how you build wealth and make your investors money. And if you are not careful, it can be what causes your demise.

Whenever you read about a company becoming "a victim of its own success," you'll find this kind of "Don't F**k It Up" culture. Companies squander their early competitive advantages and then disappear because great success in one narrowly defined area can squelch debate and foster a risk-averse mind-set among employees. The founder's comment, "Don't f**k it up," didn't really slow me down because I had known him for years and I was confident about our strategy. Most other people in the company, though, would likely take those same words to heart, as a warning from the big boss. And that can be a big problem, because employees who are taught to mistrust their own instincts are not very likely to trust their colleagues' instincts, either.

.

"Employees who are taught to mistrust their own instincts are not very likely to trust their colleagues' instincts, either."

Fear of failure can easily poison a company culture. Team-building efforts are useless when everyone's first imperative is CYA—cover your ass.

WHEN SUCCESS GOT IN THE WAY

Dominance in minicomputers made Digital Equipment Corp. (DEC) one of the most profitable companies in the world in the late 1980s. Led by Ken Olsen, its founder, DEC's minicomputers helped usher in a new era in computing, overtaking the once-dominant mainframe. In 1986 Olsen was named America's most successful entrepreneur. It wasn't long after that that Olsen forgot the lessons of his past and shielded himself from anything that might disrupt his own empire. Instead he believed that "the personal computer will fall flat on its face." Obviously, he was dead wrong. The PC flourished, with Digital Equipment missing that revolution. DEC was unceremoniously absorbed into Compaq Computer Corporation some six years later, a victim of its prior success.

Kodak was one of the world's most admired brands in 1996. Its market dominance in film enticed its out-of-touch management team to hang on to obsolete assumptions about the advantages of film-based photos over digital intruders. It might have considered letting the new generation of digital entrepreneurs within Kodak take the reins. But it never believed its empire was at risk or managed to wean itself off its revenue stream from photographic film. Kodak filed for bankruptcy liquidation in 2012, paralyzed by its past.

In 2000 Reed Hastings, the founder of what then was a fledgling company known as Netflix, had the gall to suggest a business partnership to John Antioco and his management team at Blockbuster Video. Antioco is no dummy. At the time, in fact, Antioco was viewed by many as a retail genius. But during Hastings's visit, Blockbuster was feeling pretty insular and didn't believe that this almost unknown company's innovative business model offered any value. In fact, it was reported that Hastings got laughed out of the room. Who is laughing now? Blockbuster went bankrupt in 2010, and Netflix is worth almost $70 billion.

We know there were many people inside each of these companies with bold ideas and the ability to make strategic pivots away from fading sources of revenue, but all of them were hamstrung by their leadership's choruses of "Don't f**k it up!"

"I know more about this company than anyone ever will."

The founder's attention to detail was legendary. From the time he founded his financial services software company, he was intimately involved in virtually every decision that needed to be made, and those decisions had set the stage for the company's success. He was one of those founders who could truly claim that no one knew his company as well as he did.

I came aboard to take over the role of CEO to help this founder, whom we'll call Elliot, take the company to the next level, as it was the kind of fast-growing company with strong fundamentals that could attract the interest of strategic buyers. Once I was there, though, it didn't take me long to recognize that we'd never reach our goal as long as Elliot remained the master of all detail.

One day I was talking with Elliot as we walked past the employee kitchen area when he interrupted me to point out something that had been bothering him. He'd seen tens of milk cartons of several different varieties in the refrigerator, and he wondered how we could possibly need all of this. He recalled the days when one container of regular milk would have sufficed.

I figured this was the perfect moment to set some new boundaries for Elliot's attention (even though I would have much preferred to finish our prior conversation). I told him that if he truly wanted us to succeed in the task I'd been hired for, we should never again discuss the employee kitchen. In fact, I suggested that from now on, he should try not to bother himself with any question that put less than $100,000 worth of company resources in play.

I can't ask you to stop worrying about little things. It's like telling someone not to think about pink elephants. Tiny details would always arise in your mind because your relationship to your business is so intimate. Elliot hadn't yet formulated a strategy for dealing with those thoughts. That's why the bright-line boundary of $100,000 turned out to be an excellent tool for maintaining his new focus: "Is that the exact PMS color of our logo?" Is that a $100,000 issue? No? Then forget it. Like most entrepreneurial minds, Elliot's was both voracious and decisive—as long as it had a target to hit. The $100,000 figure gave him that focus.

Drawing a bright line on such matters can be crucial to developing the mental discipline required for scaling your company. I've found that if you can develop a rule of thumb that truly resonates with you, like an arbitrary dollar figure or perhaps an organizational level ("Nothing done more than two levels below me is worth worrying about"), then you can cut way back on how much of your precious time and attention is wasted on trivia.

"If you can develop a rule of thumb that truly resonates with you, like an arbitrary dollar figure or perhaps an organizational level, then you can cut way back on how much of your precious time and attention is wasted on trivia."

That day in the employee kitchen, Elliot had interrupted what could have been an important discussion with his new CEO to ponder the company's milk expenditure. He will never know what valuable thoughts he didn't think during the minutes when he weighed the relative merits of cutting back on the milk options.

It's not easy to step back from your natural habit of having a hand in everything. You built your organization by sweating every detail, and now it feels unnatural to start ignoring those details. Then, once you truly leave those details to other people, you face yet another challenge, because those people are guaranteed to make a lot of mistakes.

LET THEM FALL, SO THAT THEY CAN SOAR

Elliot and I often discussed how, in order to meet his goals, people were going to do things in ways he'd never agree with, and some things were going to get f**ked up. But, at the risk of sounding paternalistic, the process of building a team is not that different from raising a healthy, self-sufficient child. It's not possible to be there with them constantly to ensure that they do the right thing all the time. You need to trust that with the right guidance they won't get themselves in too much trouble. And when they do get in trouble, when they fall and skin their knees, it's your role to help without being judgmental. You want them to learn from their mistakes and the resulting painful consequences.

The other important benefit of ignoring these low-level concerns is that it helps your team take over responsibility for them instead. That's how you slowly grow the decision-making muscles necessary to attain scale. The milk question was emblematic of a much larger problem at the company. Elliot's employees had helped feed his mania for details by going to him when they were making even the smallest decisions. The $100,000 mark was a helpful tool in that regard as well. He had to train himself to stop caring about countless small decisions he used to spend days obsessing over.

As a founder, it is completely natural to respond to a question posed to you by an employee or to quickly jump in to solve a tough problem. When you do, you fall into a trap. Making quick, decisive decisions is always faster, easier, and usually results in better decisions. But it encourages reliance on *you* rather than on an employee's own intellect and capabilities. Pausing to realize that not making a decision, though it may be painful, is the kind of tough love required to help employees build their own decision muscles will be an important ingredient of your organization's growth.

Mistakes can be uncomfortable to witness, and waste can feel even worse. Personally, it drives me crazy to see employees squandering company resources, whether it's the choice of an expensive hotel while traveling on business or leaving the office air-conditioning pumping all weekend. I remind them to be frugal with the accessories we purchase for our computers, subscriptions to unnecessary services, or overnight delivery when we can wait an extra day, but at the same time I try not to involve myself deeply enough in minutiae to know just how much they may or may not be wasting. If I did that, I'd be wasting two things that are much more valuable—my time and my attention.

So, instead of attempting to monitor wasteful behavior, I try my best to do what leaders are supposed to do, which is to set the tone for the entire company. The best way to promote respect for the value of company resources is to make sure you exhibit that respect yourself.

"The best way to promote respect for the value of company resources is to make sure you exhibit that respect yourself."

For instance, I make sure that my own expenses and reimbursements are more than reasonable. I don't stay at expensive hotels when traveling on business, and I often drive for six or seven hours to business destinations if flights are too expensive. And when my cell phone failed to survive a quick dip in the Severn River one day, I learned that I could save the company $600 if I waited 30 days to replace it, when my cell-phone account became upgrade-eligible.

The next morning, everyone in the office knew the reason why, for the next month, I would be using my iPad as a clumsy cell-phone substitute.

"I could have told you that would happen."

Our management team toured the battlefield at Gettysburg for a leadership exercise about how the battle was fought. We climbed up the ridgeline known as Little Round Top and paused to hear a reading of the speech that Union Colonel Joshua Chamberlain gave to his 20th Maine Regiment before the first day of battle. The monument to that regiment is one of the most popular at Gettysburg because of the famous do-or-die spirit with which the 20th held its ground.

Little Round Top sat at the extreme left flank of the Union line, and a collapse of that flank would have been disastrous for the rest of the Union Army. General Strong Vincent gave Chamberlain explicit orders to "hold this ground at all costs."

This clear statement of intent led to one of the most famously valiant episodes in the three-day battle. On the afternoon of July 3, with Confederate forces making their way up Little Round Top, Chamberlain's men ran out of ammunition. The rebels were firing their guns just 30 yards away when Chamberlain and his fellow officers led a downhill bayonet charge. A Confederate officer aimed his pistol at Chamberlain's face from a distance of just a few feet, but the gun misfired. Sharpshooters from another Union unit arrived in the nick of time to scatter the remaining Confederates.

It was nearly a religious experience for me to walk in the footsteps of the brave soldiers who fought that battle and literally changed the course of American history. The sum effect of General Vincent's clear orders, "hold this ground at all costs," motivated Chamberlain to lead his men to make a bayonet charge with no ammunition. They were told they could not afford to fail, and so they summoned the courage to succeed. Little Round Top was held, and the next day the Confederate Army retreated from Pennsylvania, never to return.

This fundamental leadership imperative, of offering clear goals and clarity of intent, is the most important tool you have in resisting your natural entrepreneurial urge to involve yourself in every little decision that affects your company. General Vincent knew he couldn't be at Little Round Top himself that day, and with no cellphone service, he entrusted Chamberlain to do his job. But he didn't leave it to Chamberlain to imagine what that job was, or what success looked like. He drew a vivid image of that day's objective—hold the hill at all costs.

On the opposite side of the battle, we learned that General Robert E. Lee was not nearly so clear in expressing his own Commander's Intent, and to this day some scholars believe the South could have won at Gettysburg and perhaps the entire war if Lee's communications to subordinates had been more explicit. The Northern defenses were centered on what was known as Cemetery Hill, and on the first day of battle Lee sent a courier to Colonel Richard Ewell with written orders to take the hill "if practicable, but to avoid a general engagement until the arrival of the other divisions of the army." Having been offered the option of waiting, Ewell decided to rest his tired troops. By the time Ewell finally attacked, on days two and three of the battle, the Northern troops were so well dug in on Cemetery Hill that the Confederate attacks were repulsed with heavy casualties.

Commander's Intent is important for precisely the reasons encountered by Chamberlain. No strategy survives encounter with the enemy.

"No strategy survives encounter with the enemy."

In business as in war, the commander is not always standing

alongside his colonel, able to change direction when his initial strategy fails. A clearly articulated intent empowers the colonel to make his own decisions without having to wait to consult with his commander—the results of which would have been disastrous for Chamberlain and the Union Army.

The Civil War generals didn't have modern communications at their disposal, so they were ultimately reliant on the judgment of their subordinates on the ground to interpret their commands. Our access to real-time communication, however, can be a trap. It tempts us to stay tethered to our organizations and to try to monitor the tiniest details—until organizational scale overwhelms us.

Founders would be much better off these days if they allowed their managers to improvise, much as Chamberlain did on Little Round Top, and use their modern communications only to provide better and clearer goals and objectives. Micromanaging can often be an excuse for not developing and committing to mid-range and long-range goals. It can also serve as an excuse, changing your mind about what's most important from one day to the next. A lot of founders run small companies that way, and they never scale those companies because it's impossible to run a larger company on the basis of what the founder is feeling that particular day.

TRUST AND VERIFY

One of the ways that a founder I know well got over micromanaging was through a phrase borrowed from Ronald Reagan: trust and verify. He worked hard to hire the right people and trusted that he'd given them the right direction to accomplish their objectives. The "verify" part involved determining what were the key indicators of success and progress toward those objectives. This is how you harness real-time data and instantaneous communication to scale your company. Agreeing on these indicators in advance enables your managers to offer you a clear line of sight to their results while keeping your nose out of their details.

It's important to be sure you pick a small subset of the right data to pay attention to. Recently, I ran into this situation at my own company. I wanted assurance that our clients' information that we store in our data cloud was arriving each night. I asked for a report that would tell me if there was an error. Instead, what I received was a long list of all of our clients and all of the data that was received by our cloud each evening, making it extremely time consuming to sift through this data for the validation I was seeking. When I pushed back, I heard groans and complaints about how all this data was necessary for those responsible to make the correct decisions. They didn't realize that I was in fact trusting them to make the right decisions and all I wanted was validation that my trust was well placed. I just wanted to know if the system worked.

One of my former board members who ran a fast-growing software company in Charleston, South Carolina, did something very similar to avoid his temptation to micromanage his sales team during a critical time when the organization was headed toward an initial public offering. The board member wanted to stay on top of how things were going, but he didn't want to be involved in every major sales transaction leading up to the IPO. So he and the sales management team agreed that he would get the following discrete information:

- average size of a transaction
- average duration of a deal through the pipeline
- number of deals entering the pipeline

- number of opportunities that entered the pipeline and converted to actual deals

He asked to be informed on an agreed-upon frequency on whether any of these metrics had begun to waver. He posted the results on the wall in his office, ensuring that his generals were keenly aware of his interest. "People respect what you inspect," he told me.

"People respect what you inspect."

The rest was left up to his team, which performed impressively and produced the desired results. The company ended up going public, and shortly thereafter the founder relinquished the CEO role to the executive formerly in charge of sales. And that successor CEO has gone on to lead yet another company.

That, in a nutshell, is the opposite of micromanaging. It might be called macro managing, but hardly anyone uses that word because there's already a better and more familiar word for it: *leadership.*

"Next time run these things past me."

I always wake early, and while indulging in my first medicinal coffee of the morning I read through email from the night before, clearing my inbox for the day ahead. One morning I noticed a celebratory email from a sales associate named Linda, announcing that an important client had signed and returned its multi-year renewal agreement. Her note exuded how she had accomplished this well in advance of our goals.

My elation over Linda's success rapidly turned to despair, however, as I read the details of the attached agreement. It was hardly a surprise that the renewal had gone through so quickly, because the agreement set our price far below that of our existing deal. Linda had not taken the time to understand the relationship with that client we had built over the past four years. By making an assumption, rather than researching the facts, she had misstated the price, and unless we fixed it, the loss would be sizeable enough to have a material impact on our annual revenue.

I just couldn't understand how this could have happened. We had gone over this specific situation the day before, and I was fully convinced that my intentions and directions were clear. I finished my coffee and got ready to head into the office. Questions ran through my mind during the drive. Should I have taken the time to check Linda's work and gone over the renewal before it went out? Was it too early in this employee's tenure to trust her to get this right?

But I also knew that to grow the organization, I would need to step back from doing things myself. When you do that, and trust people to do their jobs, inevitably some of them will breach your trust. Even if you are certain you've clearly stated your expectations and are satisfied your staff is fully trained, on some days you will be let down.

"Even if you are certain you've clearly stated your expectations and are satisfied your staff is fully trained, on some days you will be let down."

I wasn't sure what to do. I was angry and I knew that wasn't going to help. I knew there was no time for self-pity. I needed to take ownership of the damage done and make it right. In this case an important client would have to be told about the mistake and we would have to eat crow to buy back our error. In my conversations with Linda, I knew she felt awful. It was also clear that our customer was going to be disappointed. We had to undo this damage in a way that would lead to as positive an outcome as possible.

I confronted Linda as unemotionally as I could and discussed where the error had been made. There were multiple contracts that defined our relationship with this customer, and there certainly was room for confusion for someone who was not tuned in to the entire customer relationship. And then I remembered a phrase that I often use when we communicate with our clients and recited it silently to myself. "If you are communicating with someone and they don't get it, it is *your* fault, not theirs." Hearing my own words reverberate in my brain convinced me to absolve my employee from the blame. I committed to harnessing my emotion into a teachable moment.

If Linda was going to learn anything from this experience, I asked her to give me a plan on how she proposed remedying the situation. We discussed having an honest conversation with the client about what had gone wrong. We decided that we'd get the best result by addressing both our internal and external issues as directly as possible. Against my protest, Linda took ownership for both the screw-up and its remedy. Our customer turned out to be very understanding and accepted her apology, and since that episode I'm happy to say that Linda has grown in confidence and capabilities and the customer has renewed under the corrected terms.

THE IMPORTANCE OF AN
AFTER-ACTION REVIEW

After things cooled down, I brought the team together with Linda to perform an "after-action review." The term comes from the US Air Force, where teams routinely assess what they can learn from the outcomes of their most recent mission. They hold a timely, objective, no-judgment appraisal of what happened, where performance could have been better, and then collaborate on an action plan to address the areas requiring improvement. The Air Force culture is built on the assumption that the surest way to compound an error is to ignore the opportunity to learn from it.

For us, the review of the mistake took less than twenty minutes. We recognized that before we communicate with a customer, we should insert a pause and review their contract file. In that way, if there was confusion, it could be raised prior to engaging the client. The process was quite a catharsis for Linda, and it also demonstrated to everyone that while it is certainly painful to screw up, it isn't fatal. Out of this terrible mistake that had made me so angry over my morning coffee just a week earlier was a renewed *esprit de corps* in which learning from mistakes is part of our company culture. The trusting relationship we had built with the client enabled us to bridge this issue and complete the contract at the correct price.

I know of at least one company where the founder used to make mistakes a cause for celebration. He would announce mistakes that his direct reports had made in a company-wide meeting that functioned a lot like after-action reviews. They were intended to identify how and why the underlying decision went wrong, in order to make meaning of the resulting failure. The founder usually made certain to compliment the effort that led to the error—making it clear that trying new things in the face of risk was vital to the company's growth.

Promoting a culture that encourages risk taking, questioning the status quo, and even challenging the company founder is the best prescription for healthy growth. You want to embrace the kind of executives who have enough guts to call your baby ugly if that's how they see it. Exhibiting the confidence to bring others into your organization who might just disagree with you is a critical ingredient of scaling.

"Exhibiting the confidence to bring others into your organization who might just disagree with you is a critical ingredient of scaling."

There are many strong-willed founders who can't tolerate this kind of environment, much to their detriment. Too many founders with early success develop a belief system that they know better than anyone, that they are always right—right enough to stop soul searching or listening to others. Founders of this kind often protect their fragile egos by hiring friends and family members who don't dare question the boss, because they know their main function is to exercise loyalty, not competence. Then, when a mistake happens, the founder can't possibly hold an open and honest review of the problem because it might expose the ineffectiveness of his loyal inner circle. The overall effect—one that smells a lot like hubris— can sow the seeds of doubt and dysfunction throughout the organization, and inevitably lead to the founder's downfall.

TWO

SEEKING HIGHER GROUND

"We'll never find someone who can do this as well as me."

A CEO colleague of mine we'll call Jack had personally run the sales functions at his company, among his many other duties, ever since the founding of his fast-growing software and services firm. Jack kept the lead sales role because he was really good at it. For most of five years, sales had grown at a compounded annual rate approaching 50 percent until just a few years ago, when he finally handed off the job to someone else.

His replacement was not nearly as impressive at running the sales operation. "Our head of sales is good," Jack told me. "But he has some noticeable shortcomings. His focus on process and getting his team to assess their deals objectively leads to too many surprises, when deals he forecasted end up not closing during the quarter. He's not nearly as good at cutting through the bullshit that salespeople often conjure up during their pipeline reviews."

Nonetheless, Jack avoided the temptation to lean in or try to help out. "Even if he is just 80 percent as good as me at some of these things, I would never undercut him."

Besides, Jack told me, even if he wanted to undercut his head of sales, he doesn't have the time or attention to spare. Jack's sales prowess had catapulted the company into a crowded and competitive space, one where simple organic growth through increased sales is now not enough to ensure the company's competitiveness. So Jack needed to shift his CEO focus from sales, where he excelled, to bulking up the company through acquisitions, something he initially knew almost nothing about. He urgently needed to build a team to help him identify acquisition opportunities before better-financed competitors swooped in and ate his lunch. The threat was so clear to Jack that he knew it was time to turn over the sales leadership role to someone else.

Jack is lucky because the market spoke so clearly to him. He risked losing everything if he didn't give up an important job he'd always done himself. Most founders never get this message handed to them the way Jack did. When you began your company, you were required to do just about everything. But as you continued to scale, there was a crying need for specialists to handle tasks that had become full-time roles, not functions you could handle with your time and attention divided.

Founders experience this natural tension in almost everything they do—holding tight to tasks that make them comfortable, ones that reside in their sweet spots of ability and help them maintain a sense of control over the business. Gravitating toward things that we know how to do well is a human trait. We crave being good at something and the ensuing praise and positive reinforcement. And when we find that thing, we naturally repeat it with increasing strengthening of our skill. If you want to scale your business, however, you must challenge this natural tendency. You need to look critically at everything you do and ask, is this the right thing? Is it the most important thing? Is there someone else I could find who could do this thing just as well or even better than me?

And then, most critically, the issue arises: what if I can't find that person? Is 80 percent proficiency good enough? Jack understood that he had an urgent need to go this step further and surrender control over sales to someone not nearly as good as him. That's a very difficult step to take, but often the alternative is worse. As a colleague of mine told me that he learned early in his founder experience, it's usually better to let someone else get something done 80 percent as well as you would have done it—just so you can focus on far more important matters.

"It's usually better to let someone else get something done 80 percent as well as you would have done it— just so you can focus on far more important matters."

There is a natural tendency of a founder to grab functions and control tasks. To punctuate this point at Transcentive, we engaged Lynn Giuliani, an executive coach, to facilitate a company offsite. She led us through an exercise focused on teamwork and delegation. Lynn divided the senior management team into groups. Each group was composed of several people who were not permitted to speak, a group leader who was not permitted to see, and several others not permitted to use their hands. Then she placed a box of Legos on the floor in front of the group leader, the one who was blindfolded. The goal was to build a house out of these Legos.

When the exercise commenced, I watched in awe as the blind-folded founder immediately spread his arms wide and accumulated all the Legos he could by touch and feel alone. With no help from his teammates who literally had clear sight of the goal, he began to architect the entire structure himself. The rest of the team stood around dumbfounded. His behavior was emblematic of the challenge for this company as it was poised to grow.

Maybe Jack's admission that there might be someone to do the job 80 percent as well as he could is a fiction that he needed to create in his own mind to avoid the inevitable truth—there might just be someone who can do something better. Because believe me, there are people out there who are much more specialized and experienced that can handle some of your functions better than you. It's time for you to realize that the value you bring to your organization has nothing to do with how well you do any one specific function. It's about your vision, drive, and leadership. Despite your natural reluctance and ego, giving up individual tasks to others is your first step up The Founder Value Ladder.

If decades of experience managing businesses and mentoring CEOs has taught me anything, it's that your most important challenge as a founder is to continuously and relentlessly seek opportunities to give up task-oriented functions and delegate them to others. The mark of a successful founder is to shed individual contributor tasks you excel at in order to make more room for thinking and planning. If you step back further and further from doing and move closer and closer to being your firm's head visionary, you will inevitably become superfluous to day-to-day operations. That's when you've truly created a valuable business, one that has value in the capital markets or is desirable to a buyer—because it's an organization that can succeed with *or* without you.

"It's better if I do this myself."

I still own the day-to-day accounting responsibilities at Purview, despite my constant worry that this is not the best use of my time. I tell myself I will only do this until we can afford to hire someone else to do it full-time, but I'm not sure I will ever feel like giving it up. Being close to the financial accounts connects me with the business in a way that nothing else can. It gives me intimate knowledge of how we are doing and, above all, it feels comfortable.

But I also know that handing off daily accounting duties is next on my list of things to do in order for our organization to grow. *Doing* is a personal experience that doesn't scale. Breaking out of this box is the difference between founders who transition and those who don't. I know that I have to bring in someone else and train her, which is time consuming, but in that sense it's time to slow down to speed up.

Without a coach constantly by your side, it's often difficult for a founder to be self-reflective on how you spend your day. I've adopted a four-step process that I have found to be an invaluable guide to founders to help them prioritize their activities:

1. **Track your time.** For just one week, keep a timesheet and write down how you spend every hour (it's even better if you

do this for a month). As the CEO, you want to spend no more than half your time on tactical, day-to-day issues. The bulk of your time, at least 50 percent, should be spent on strategic planning, dealing with the core issues that you've identified as your top priorities with your direct reports. Tracking your time will reveal to you just how much of what you do is aligned with scaling the organization. You may be quite surprised at your results.

2. **Decide what not to work on,** and stick to it. Something's got to go if you want to get your strategic activities above 50 percent. Allowing a few pet projects, like putting your personal touches on the annual company meeting or editing that customer email, has to burn to the ground (or more likely get done by someone else who will probably do a fine job on them) to ultimately provide you with the time you need to work *on* your business and not *in* it. Then use your timesheet to help hold yourself accountable.

3. **Plan for the unexpected.** A retired Navy SEAL once told me: "If you have only one alternative course of action, you have none. If you have two, you really only have one." In other words, for every important contingency, make sure you always have a Plan B and a Plan C—a backup to the backup. Surprises are inevitable, but being unprepared is inexcusable. Think deeply about what might occur, in your business and your life, and put some plans in place for a range of potential outcomes. Giving yourself more time for strategic planning allows you to avoid scrambling and being caught unaware when the unexpected happens.

4. **Write down your goals and revisit them quarterly**. Out of this process you might see that you're not as clear about your

assumed goals as you thought. Write down your goals. There's an old saying in business: "If it isn't written down, it doesn't exist." Then find a prominent place in your office to post them and make sure you share them with your team. Use your goals to drive behavior and decision-making—not the latest email.

These four steps offer you a chance to develop new positive habits and help you break the old habit of wanting to handle things yourself. We are all creatures of habit. When I balance the books, I'm in my comfort zone. I know how to do it. I am good at it. And I crave it. But checking the finances has now become a bad habit, no different than any other bad habit you'd care to mention. I do it even though I know I'd be better off doing something more important and productive with my time.

REDUCE YOUR CLUTTER—APPOINT A GUARD DOG

One of the ways to begin to wean yourself from tasks that don't require your expertise and authority is to designate someone other than yourself to be your guard dog. In many founder-led organizations, when an issue arises that doesn't fit anyone's area of responsibility, dealing with the issue usually defaults to the founder. Issues of this kind can clog the founder's day with small and inconsequential matters. Choosing one person for the job of protecting you from these distractions will go a long way toward unclogging your calendar, making room for your target of 50 percent reserved for strategic planning.

In general, successful founders are those who can learn to pride themselves on reducing clutter of all kinds—the *feng shui* of your new existence.

"In general, successful founders are those who can learn to pride themselves on reducing clutter of all kinds—the feng shui *of your new existence."*

When it comes to email correspondence or interruptions, think quality over quantity and wean yourself from the constant barrage of interruptions. Founders often find that even a small reduction in email volume begins to worry them as they start to delegate a few of their responsibilities. Does it mean they are losing their importance?

Like most founders, you have ultimate confidence in yourself, so sharing responsibility will likely never come naturally to you. Also, like most founders, you've been operating in a host of varied functions for quite some time with very positive results, so a do-it-yourself habit may appear to be one of your more admirable qualities. Bad habits are hard enough to break. Productive habits, habits that produce positive results in the short term, are even harder to break. Meanwhile, the new habits of delegation and decluttering that you're trying to develop are not going to make you feel comfortable at all. Some will feel terrible.

Knowing this is not the same as understanding it. If you look up a video called *The Backwards Brain Bicycle,* you'll see a powerful demonstration of how hard it is for your brain to adjust to a new way of doing even the simplest of tasks, one that is seemingly fully understandable.

Destin Sandlin, an aerospace engineer who hosts a video series called *Smarter Every Day,* rigged up a bicycle with a special gear between the handlebars and the front wheel so that turning the handlebars to the right would make the front wheel turn left, and vice versa. In the eight-minute video, you see how this single modification makes bike riding impossible. Even though Sandlin told himself over and over to steer right to go left, he could not get his hands to cooperate with the new instructions and kept falling off the bicycle. All the ingrained behaviors from a lifetime of bike riding were simply too strong to overcome through sheer willpower. Even though he knew the bicycle would go left when he steered right, it took him eight months to understand how to ride the bike well enough to master the new habit.

The Backwards Brain Bicycle offers one other lesson. Once Sandlin had finally trained himself to ride the Backwards Bicycle, the change in Sandlin's brain was still extremely fragile. It took all his focus and concentration to maintain his balance on the Backwards Bicycle. The slightest distraction—the ring of his cell phone, for instance—would send Sandlin's mind back to his old habitual way of steering and send Sandlin's body tumbling off the Backwards Bicycle. Stress, deadlines, and distractions are bound to have the same effect on your new habits of delegation, always threatening to throw you back into the familiar habit of handling all the details yourself, starving your true priorities of your time and attention.

"Next time I'll let someone else handle it."

The members of the marketing team faced a serious dilemma. The company's website was in desperate need of a revamp to attract more leads. But the time they would need to invest in fixing the website would inevitably take them away from some of their other important lead-generation activities. Taking their eyes off lead generation might cut into their monthly metrics, but the old website was so outdated that they were sure they were wasting many of the new leads they were generating.

It was a clear trade-off. One function or the other was bound to suffer, and no one wanted to take responsibility for choosing which one. They were used to asking the founder to make these types of calls. So they met with the founder and asked him to tell them what to do.

"It's a tough choice, I know," he told them. He went over the details with the group, and they held their collective breath as they awaited his marching orders. He was a classic market-focused take-charge CEO. Normally, his inclination was to make the decision before they'd finished describing the problem, but this time he quietly and thoughtfully pushed back.

"Let me know which way you choose," he said.

It was a small step, but it represented a total about-face in terms of direction. Months later, this meeting could be seen as a critical turning point in the relationship between the founder and the marketing team. With time, the marketing team grew more acclimated to making important choices on their own, and the founder grew more comfortable not weighing in or more realistically preempting decisions simply because he'd always done so.

As you begin to peel back your own responsibilities and focus on what not to be involved with, you inevitably disrupt the decision flow in the organization and push your employees out of their own comfort zones. Some might feel abandoned and get angry over the new responsibilities you're giving them. Others will experience fear and anguish that they're being set up to take blame for something that might not work. Their prior intimate reliance on the founder seems to be giving way to a less familiar and more institutional process, one that requires them to step up, accept responsibility, but leave the comfort of their cocoon.

Shortly after I had taken over responsibility for sales at one company, the CFO stopped by my office to let me know that she had found an anonymous note that had been strategically dropped on the floor outside her office. The note complained bitterly about the new expectations I'd set for sales executives and suggested that I didn't know what I was doing. Actually the note was a lot more graphic than that. Although many employees embraced the new performance measures I'd introduced as a way of helping them stand out and prove themselves, there were a few who felt threatened and angry by the change. Over time, however, the benefits became obvious, managers developed new capabilities as a result, and the new system made it easier to weed out weaker players—if they didn't leave of their own accord first.

At the same time, there are ways a founder might delegate tasks irresponsibly, in which case employees have a right to be mad. You must make sure that when you transfer these functions to others, those people are both capable and empowered to complete their jobs. Sounds simple, but some founders have an ugly character flaw in which they delegate responsibilities but withhold authority. The relationship between responsibility and authority needs to be hand in glove.

"The relationship between responsibility and authority needs to be hand in glove."

Founders need to be willing to grant both together or neither at all, and then live by that. There is no partway. The least bit of gap between the two will be sufficient for astute and sometimes motivated employees to drive an expensive truck through.

With responsibility goes authority. There will be people within your organization who will not be comfortable with others owning responsibility for things that used to be in your domain. Just like my anonymous note, they will try to undermine the new authority and make those people look bad in the process. You will need to go out of your way to ensure that this doesn't happen. The true test of a founder investing others with authority is when they are able to solve issues without needing to consult back with the founder. There is simply no other way to improve decision-making cycle times in a way that helps the organization grow and scale.

In a former role as the CEO of a growing technology company, I had a great employee, whom we'll call Karen. Karen was conscientious, smart, and worked extremely hard. Like many good employees, she was always busy, whether running a meeting, calling a customer, or putting out a fire. I sensed that the hours she was working were physically taking their toll. I knew it was time to try to help or risk losing her to burnout.

One day we sat down for an update and I asked Karen if she knew why she seemed to be so much busier than I am. She said she didn't. I already knew the answer that I was eager to share with her.

"'Because,' I explained, "I have you working for me—and you don't.'"

Karen got it instantly. She acknowledged that too much of her time was spent responding to emergencies. It's good to be responsive (and responsible), but on days when her time was consumed by stamping out fires, she did little to grow the capacity of her team and develop new strategies that might cut down on the number of fires needing to be stamped out.

I challenged Karen to find her own trustworthy lieutenant and spend less time responding to the latest urgency and more time on planning. At first, it was difficult for her to find her own Karen. It was only after several unsuccessful months of recruiting that she realized that a candidate who was 80 percent as good as she was would do just fine. And with her mentoring, that person quickly scaled her capabilities.

Karen ultimately built a world-class team and went on to become a successful founder herself. She found that while it had been a real rush putting out fires herself, it was much more fulfilling to enable and train others to rise to the occasion. I hope she's passed on the same advice I offered her that day.

"I think you might want to reconsider what you are about to do."

A colleague called me one evening for advice. He had recently promoted his head of sales into the role of CEO, and now that new CEO was headed toward a train wreck. What should he do? As a founder in a mentoring role, shouldn't he try to protect his CEO from himself?

The issue was the new CEO's first strategic plan for the company. Not long after his promotion, the new CEO worked on it intensely by himself, assuming it would give his executive team a blueprint for the company's direction. But the plan was long and detailed. It ran well more than fifty pages and was so exhaustive in its recommendations that everyone would recognize instantly that it was unworkable. If anything, all the plan would accomplish would be to expose how raw the new CEO really was.

The founder had seen it coming as the CEO toiled away preparing the document. It took all the restraint he had in him, but the founder avoided telling his successor what he thought, that good strategic plans deal in short, bold strokes and are best drafted in consultation with the executive team. It had been agonizing for him to see the plan grow in size and complexity, and now, before following his impulse to jump in and save his successor from embarrassment, my colleague called to ask me if a last-minute intervention was really the right thing to do.

You can probably guess my response. There are many things your successor can only learn by screwing them up and then fixing them, I told him. This is clearly one of them. As I saw it, any damage done to the company would be minimal and temporary. The new CEO would get valuable training by stumbling, falling, and then working through the problem he created on his own. It might do him good to be seen as human right from the start.

Then we shifted the conversation to my true concern. I wanted to hear from my friend how difficult it was going to be for him to stand by while this slow-motion train wreck unfolded. We weighed the consequences of keeping out of it, and determined that the risk/reward equation was sound. My friend stepped back and watched the crash and its aftermath. Despite some consequences, he was pleased to see the CEO quickly acknowledge the mistake. The lesson was clear. The authority bestowed on him was also clear. The fire wall the founder had built to ensure that he did not interfere was intact. The new CEO led the company for several more years and grew it until its ultimately very successful sale. He then went on to take the reins of another company, one in which his former founder was first in line to invest.

We learn more from mistakes than from successes.

"We learn more from mistakes than from successes."

As a founder focused on growth and scale, the more you can enable these teachable moments without jumping in, the faster and more easily your team will expand their capabilities and capacities for leadership. If you are a parent, you already know this lesson. It's like trying to teach your kid to ride a two-wheeler without her suffering any cuts and bruises on her legs from her first wobbly ventures. Those *strawberries* are (hopefully) a small price to pay for her ultimate success.

ONE THROAT TO CHOKE

The secret to getting used to delegation is to keep thinking small. Distribute authority to a set of small groups with clear ownership responsibility. Then make sure there is a single person in each group you can call upon to ensure the task is handled.

While this seems obvious, there is a tremendous temptation for founders to focus on making people happy, including themselves, by designating co-chairs for committees or offering employees overlapping responsibilities. All too often I've seen founders designate their successor as a co-president or co-CEO, a situation that is surely going to confuse your employees as to who is in charge. Unfortunately, your unwillingness to let go completely, to make organization charts crystal clear, and to make the tough calls that might offend a former peer of your new CEO is how you invite hard questions to go unasked, dysfunctions to not be addressed, and important matters to fall like hot potatoes.

Instead, you want to give one person the domain over his group and hold him responsible for the results. Doing so will go a long way toward you releasing your grip on things you can't really control anyway.

"One throat to choke" is what I like to call this principle, in the most affectionate way.

So instead of withholding work you're not sure your team is up to, perhaps you should let them know that this work is a stretch, and that they should go in with the attitude of making mistakes quickly—of course not purposefully, but with ritualistic processes to ensure that you all learn from these mistakes. After-action reviews enable institutional learning from situations just like this. The saying goes that it's not that you fall down but it is how you get up. The parallel is that it's not how your team fails that matters as much as how you respond in helping them up.

> "It's not how your team fails that matters as much as how you respond in helping them up."

That will truly enable your team to grow in the most expeditious fashion.

And then, the only remaining way for you to screw things up is to obey the temptation to pull rank every now and then, and do an end run around the system you've set up. Nothing is more dispiriting to a team than to have a do-as-I-say-not-as-I-do boss, but most founders I've known feel they must occasionally step in personally and take back responsibility they've delegated, at least on an ad hoc basis. The result is almost never good.

I fell prey to exactly this type of situation that could have and should have been avoided. As the newly appointed successor CEO to a founder, I found it necessary to part with a long-term company executive. The founder and this vice president (call him Ted) had been quite close for years. But it was clear (to almost everyone in the company) that Ted was no longer right for his role as the company had grown, and there was no practical way to reassign him to another role. I knew this would be tough on the founder, so having talked over the situation with him, I took responsibility for approaching Ted with the bad news and a severance package ready.

However, before I did, I also asked the founder to promise he would not undermine me in Ted's termination. I expected that once I had met with Ted, he would go straight to the founder seeking a reprieve. I felt it was important that the founder back me up and tell Ted that the severance package was very generous (it certainly was!) and that the decision was entirely mine.

Unfortunately, as I feared, when Ted ran to the founder, the founder's resolve melted in the presence of a long-term employee with whom he had a long, emotional relationship. The founder sweetened the severance package significantly, even though he described it to me as "just a little." The size of the severance package, which included a buyback of the vice president's stock options, was enough to taint our valuation—and hence the market value of the stock options we had just granted. That sweetened severance package ended up costing us millions of dollars in unnecessary taxes. "Just a little" was also sufficient to signal to everyone else at the company that my authority was incomplete, which eventually impacted my tenure with the company. "Just a little" ended up costing the company and me quite a lot.

One throat to choke. 80 percent. Backwards Bicycle. Remember these three principles, and that's really all you need to know about delegation.

THREE

THEY'RE EXPECTING ME

"That customer and I have a long-standing relationship."

As the vice president of operations at an early-stage software company, I was well aware that the founder, whom we'll call Sandra, had developed some very valuable and deeply personal customer relationships among major firms in our particular industry. The leaders at these firms regarded Sandra highly, finding her both genial and trustworthy. Deepening and expanding these relationships was critical to the company's future, and it was a task Sandra shouldered almost entirely on her own.

Then, a festering problem began to develop with one of these customers. We had fallen far behind schedule in delivering a valuable custom feature we had promised. Things were getting strained between our company and the customer, and I could see what the true underlying problem was. Sandra was too embarrassed to go directly to the client and come clean about the situation. A complicating factor was that she wasn't confident she could explain what had gone wrong in the schedule, because the company's products had grown so complex.

When I finally offered to step in and confront the problem with the customer, Sandra was nervous about the idea. But she was also relieved. It was clear that the more successful we were, the larger and more complex these relationships were becoming. This terrible problem was an opportunity to extend this customer relationship beyond having just the CEO/founder as the company's face. Predictably, she warned me, "Don't f**k it up."

In my visit with the customer, I took personal responsibility for the extended delay. I also admitted that I couldn't predict when we'd be able to deliver, so I offered the customer the opportunity to withdraw from our contract without a penalty. As it turned out, the customer was willing to stick with us through the delay because they still trusted that we offered the best solution available. We had the frank and straightforward conversation that had been needed months earlier, one that Sandra had been putting off because she was too personally invested in the customer relationship. The customer appreciated my honesty, and a new relationship between the company and the customer was born—a relationship that was no longer solely dependent on the founder's direct involvement with the account.

Beyond keeping an important customer happy, the best thing about this incident was that within the organization we had finally set a precedent for cutting the cord between the founder and an important customer. Each relationship with every major customer had been painstakingly initiated and negotiated by Sandra. No one in the company knew anything about all the provisional verbal commitments Sandra might have obligated the company to perform for these accounts.

This had to change if the company was ever going to scale. And it had to change before we faced yet another crisis with an unhappy customer.

As your venture grows, it will be impractical for you to have a personal relationship with every customer. So learning this lesson and getting comfortable letting others take over your relationships and develop some of their own without you is a critical ingredient to your growth.

> *"As your venture grows, it will be impractical for you to have a personal relationship with every customer."*

As I mentioned in the introduction, scaling your company will require you to evolve as a leader. While your charisma, industry relationships (we used to call this a Rolodex), and technical knowledge may have been instrumental to your venture's initial success, they will hold you back from reaching the next level. If you want to be the one to head your organization as it transcends its next growth phase, you must successively take on more advanced roles, climbing what I call The Founder Value Ladder™ as you shed old roles that are no longer appropriate for you.

The rungs of The Founder Value Ladder look like this:

INVESTOR
ARCHITECT
STRATEGIST
COACH
PLAYER

As you scale the ladder, your value to the organization grows. The ladder gets narrower at the top; there is not room for too many others in your organization to stand on the upper rungs. And in fact, not every founder can keep their balance as they scale these heights. These are the rungs of organizational leadership.

RICH OR KING:
CLIMBING THE FOUNDER VALUE LADDER

Every founder starts at the bottom of the ladder. They bring new storefronts to a stodgy industry like Jeff Bezos at Amazon, a new approach to sales channels like Michael Dell at his eponymously named computer company, create new product categories like Steve Jobs at Apple, or new styles like Diane von Fürstenberg. But you would never have heard about any of those executives if they had all remained on the ladder's bottom rung.

The idea for this ladder was introduced to me by Mark Helow, the founder of a CEO peer group then known as Inc. Eagles. Mark described the ladder as a path for the increasing value of your contributions to your organization. What stuck with me from this ladder analogy was that although moving up the ladder seems directionally correct, not every founder is willing or capable of climbing all the way to the top. And getting to the top should not be the singular goal of every founder.

There are many successful founders who actually never made it above the first rung. Most of those are not household names. Many made plenty of money and created important enterprises, but only after giving way to other capable leaders. People like Leonard Bosack and his wife, Sandy Lerner, who founded Cisco but were ultimately succeeded by John Chambers, and Martin Eberhard, who cofounded Tesla Motors, not with Elon Musk but with another unknown, Marc Tarpenning. And, in my direct experience, Bob Thomson, founder of Hyperion Solutions (then known as IMRS, Inc.), who gave way to Jim Perakis.

As a founder, you must realize that there is no sin in sticking to the first rung or getting off the ladder early. It can often be the most direct path to maximizing your wealth. But it's a choice that every founder has to make. Noam Wasserman, formerly of the Harvard Business School, calls this choice *rich* or *king*. He argues that optimizing results for founders requires that they make the binary choice between maximizing their wealth or maximizing their stature. For those not willing or perhaps not skilled in climbing the ladder, the choice of *rich* means getting off the ladder early. Sometimes this choice is made for you, as happened to Bosack and Lerner, who were relegated to a measly $170 million payday, selling their Cisco stock when they were forced out of their company by their investors.

To climb the ladder, you must be willing to reinvent yourself on almost every rung. We started this journey in Chapter One by not meddling in responsibilities that belong to others. Chapter Two was about being a better coach, by teaching others to take on responsibilities that had once been yours. This chapter involves grasping the next rung of the ladder, as a strategist. This newest role requires you to devote more of your time and attention to making bigger decisions that take the long view of your company's future.

And in order to succeed at this new strategist stage, you must surrender your former role as a player and even some of that as a coach. Despite what you may currently think, you can train or hire others to take on some of your former tasks. To climb the value ladder, you have to give up much of your hands-on work. Someone other than you should be handling your most critical sales prospects and their support calls. The features of your new product need to be handed off to a designer. Someone else should be managing the relationship with your accountants.

What I find so helpful about The Founder Value Ladder is that it illustrates an important principle: You can only be effective while occupying at most two adjacent ladder rungs at a time. If you want to seize the strategist rung, you must step off the player rung—and among other things, that means no more direct interference with customer accounts.

"You can only be effective while occupying at most two adjacent ladder rungs at a time."

If the coaching rung is all about delegating many of your old responsibilities to others, then the strategist rung begins by delegating many of your old relationships to others. You can tell yourself that customers expect you to show up for them and hold their hand, just as you did when your company was small. But you can't scale the company on that basis. If you believe that you are a critical player in every new sale, then your venture is destined to fail. You must accept that maintaining your exclusive close contact with top customers is limiting and will wind up doing more harm than good—to yourself, to your people, to your organization and, as we'll see, even to the customers who crave your attention.

Every company needs subject matter experts. These are the

players. Most founders' original value comes at this rung of the ladder. Many end up staying there. Which is no sin; it's just not leadership.

As we move through the remaining chapters of this book, you will find yourself being nudged up the rungs toward architect and investor. Each requires you to give up some of your former behaviors, especially the ones that have grown so comfortable. But as the remaining chapters point out, it is impossible to climb to the leadership heights required by your growing venture without letting go of a lower rung. Deciding how high to try to climb is one of the most critical decisions for a founder to make.

"I'll just take this customer's call."

I've worked with some very capable founders who had been personally and intimately involved in sales to many of their early customers. One situation in particular involved a client who had a habit of calling the founder on his cell phone whenever there were problems with the software. Even after we'd established a service desk, it was difficult to break this customer's routine practice of calling the founder directly. That's probably because whenever the customer complained to the founder, the founder dutifully dropped everything he was doing and took care of the customer's request. Admirable, but not scalable behavior.

This pattern continued as the company grew and the founder became busier, until one day, inevitably, a customer called, the founder promised action—and then completely forgot to follow through. Since the founder had taken the call on his cell phone while he was in his car, he also neglected to log the call in our CRM (customer relationship management) system, so no one else in the company was aware of this customer's issue. Six months later, that customer called the founder for the very last time—to let him know they were leaving for a competitor.

In the wake of losing this customer, we instituted an after-action review to determine how to improve our system. The founder's version of the story was that he didn't want to offend his long-term customers by telling them they should stop calling him directly. Again, admirable but not scalable. He also said he feared the customer would object if he passed them off to what they viewed as a lower-level employee in customer support. At the same time, the founder had to admit that in this case, his fear of offending the customer had resulted in worse service and the loss of a long-term account. Everyone would have been better served, including the customer, if he'd followed protocol and taken steps to wean the customer off the habit of calling him directly.

If you're being honest with yourself, it's fairly easy to proactively transition a customer's account to someone else in the company without offending that customer. Most founders are good salespeople, and they certainly would know how to sell a customer on the benefits of having someone other than their distracted selves handling the account. It's also not that hard to explain to your customers that they would be better served by dealing with the help desk, where trained professionals are far more up to date in their technical expertise. Where their issues will be recorded, scrutinized on a timely basis, and escalated if not addressed. If the customer is really important, it's a fairly simple matter to take that customer to lunch and introduce their new contact, ideally someone who also has much more direct knowledge of how your systems are working.

This advice is so simple and practical that if you can't follow through on it, then you have to confront a deeper problem within yourself. You must come to grips with the fact that you've got an unhealthy emotional attachment to your importance to your customers. You may tell yourself this early customer deserves to hear from you directly, but what truly deserves your focus and undivided attention is your job of taking your company to the next level of growth.

"You may tell yourself this early customer deserves to hear from you directly, but what truly deserves your focus and undivided attention is your job of taking your company to the next level of growth."

Yes, you may love your long-term customers, but there comes a point when that good loving's gone bad.

AVOID HAVING A SINGLE POINT OF FAILURE

At one company I know, the founder had long ago been an employee at a firm that is now one of his major clients. Ten years after setting off on his own, the founder still maintains a deeply personal relationship with this client firm. He takes support calls on his cell phone from his former colleagues there. He'll drop what he is doing to run over to the customer's site to solve one of their issues, because it feels a little like homecoming when he goes back there. His former colleagues are always happy to see him, hear about his growing family, and get caught up on the latest developments in his life. Despite all the new demands on his time and attention over these past ten years, the founder believes that his original client is still so important to the company that it deserves to hear from him when they need him.

That's commendable, right? Maybe, but it's also self-indulgent and extremely limiting. By now, the founder has such a complete, unique, and personal knowledge of this client's systems that if something were to happen to him, his employees wouldn't know what to do to help the client. That should really concern the client, whose operations are highly dependent on his software. The client has grown so reliant on this one personal relationship that if something were to go haywire with the software, so many custom modifications have been done on an undocumented "friendly" basis that neither party can identify where their respective legal contractual responsibilities begin and end. This is a very unhealthy situation for both the founder and his client firm. It's almost bound to end badly unless one or the other insists on a change. By not letting go of the bottom rung of the ladder, the founder made it clear that he would need someone else to climb the remaining rungs of The Founder Value Ladder for him.

I sit on the board of a company that had a sales territory manager who acted in a similar way. You probably are familiar with situations like this, perhaps at your current company. She treated her clients with personal attention. Few people in her division, let alone throughout the company, knew the ins and outs of her account like she did. Her manager viewed her relationship with this large account as critically important to its retention. Unfortunately, when she inevitably left the company, the account went out the door with her. In retrospect, her manager realized that his reluctance to institutionalize the company's contact with that client was shortsighted and risky. Developing rapport with a customer can be important; but maintaining only a single point of contact can certainly become a single point of failure. This is an important lesson for any founder who personally handles his own accounts.

"Developing rapport with a customer can be important; but maintaining only a single point of contact can certainly become a single point of failure."

DETOXING YOUR CUSTOMERS' RELIANCE

In order to institutionalize your customer relationships in a way that's consistent with being a scalable company, you first have to detox these types of relationships with customers. Put together a step-by-step strategic approach for handing off customers to others at the company, and start with the ones who are the highest maintenance and most distracting to you, the founder. You can do this by methodically introducing some of your colleagues into these accounts until they too develop trusted relationships with these clients. Then slowly withdraw yourself from directly interacting with these accounts.

The customers who are the closest ones to you are the ones that are most dangerous and need to be put at arm's-length soonest, because they are the ones most responsible for sapping your time and energy as well as the most at-risk if you are gone. If you can wean them off their connection with you—and wean yourself off your connection with them—you'll take a very important step up the ladder toward aligning your daily priorities with your long-term goals and the value that can come from gaining a higher perspective on your business.

"I don't have time to record all this stuff in our system."

Managing the transition in your privileged relationship with a customer is much easier if you're transitioning them to something you know is set up to be more responsive and more reliable. That isn't very hard to do if you get a system in place and then staff it and use it properly. Installing a CRM system or upgrading the one you currently have is another one of those infrastructure items that may slow you down in the short run but sets you up for long-term success. It's one more case of slowing down in order to speed up your rate of scale.

The process of transferring all this information into a system rarely goes cleanly. Within the organization, it often uncovers some unpleasant secrets and procedural inadequacies that are embarrassing ("Why can't you find that customer's contract?"). These are common unstated reasons why staff members may resist making the shift, so it will be up to you to insist on it. The main objective is to seize the opportunity to wean the customers from the founder, the salesperson we discussed in the prior chapter, or any single individual and institutionalize the process of managing the accounts going forward. Keep in mind that if a contract or some other vital document is missing, now is the perfect time to recognize it and address the problem—not later, after a deal goes bad and you go scrambling for protection from a document that doesn't exist. A colleague of mine who used to work for Goldman Sachs once reminded me that contrary to popular opinion, "There actually are stupid questions. But a stupid question today if not asked now is an even stupider question later."

"A stupid question today if not asked now is an even stupider question later."

Asking where the contract is today is one of those stupid questions. But asking *now* is the right thing to do.

I've witnessed at least one instance where a troublesome customer called with what would be a complicated product issue. Of course the call went right to the founder (his cell phone was the only number the customer had). As the founder scurried to initiate a fire drill, I overheard the conversation and dug into our records to find that this particular customer's support contract had run out. It felt much better for us to be allocating resources to the emergency when in return we received a lucrative multi-year support contract extension.

I've joked with a founder before that his next vacation was dependent on his ability to document all of his customer contacts before he leaves. Otherwise, he could expect to be interrupted by calls from our support team trying to parse through his personal customer interactions. I've personally taken an escalated support call from an early client who refused to follow our established process. He complained that several of his support issues had not yet been resolved. It turned out (no surprise!) that his calls went directly to the founder and were never recorded. I assured him that if he would use the process, everything in our CRM would be up to date, and that it would be easier and faster for him to get his problems resolved. I still doubt he will follow my advice, but at least I felt better about why he had unresolved issues.

BUILDING INSTITUTIONAL KNOWLEDGE

That's why, once the system is in place, it's just as important to police its usage. And despite this process being antagonistic to most founders' DNA, you need to set a clear example. The mandatory logging of all customer interactions must become a firm rule. From an organizational standpoint, if any interaction isn't entered in the system, it's as though it never happened—like the forgotten phone call from the customer that resulted in the loss of that customer. If it isn't written down, it doesn't exist. Stuff that is only stored between the ears of one human being is just too much of a risk for a growing organization.

> *"Stuff that is only stored between the ears of one human being is just too much of a risk for a growing organization."*

Maintaining a process for recording customer interactions, like support calls, is an area that often gets overlooked early in an organization's evolution, and this is your opportunity to get that behavior under control.

The purpose of a system such as this, as with all documentation, is to build the institutional knowledge of the organization. Anyone new to the company should be able to open a customer file and know when they were last contacted, what they bought, what they paid, what the ongoing responsibilities of the company are to the customer, and any issues he or she has raised, as well as their contract's expiration date. At Purview, our process includes proactively contacting each of our customers at least once a quarter, just to see how they are doing. We meticulously record this information in our system. Two months before renewal time, we make sure to contact them again and use the CRM to recite back all the value they received (calls that were resolved, issues that were identified, things we'd jumped through hoops to provide). This has improved our customer renewals by more than a double-digit percentage!

Although I've seen some companies regard documentation as an optional step for account managers, that's a risky policy to follow. When you write this stuff down, it becomes tangible. Now is the time to consider that future investors will look to the strength and integrity of all your systems as a big factor in determining what your company is actually worth. Even future hires will have more respect for the company and its culture if they find the company systems are strong and reliable. Having historical customer information at their fingertips instills a confidence right from the start. There's a lot more at stake in running your CRM well than just improved customer relationships.

"There's a lot more at stake in running your CRM well than just improved customer relationships."

As your organization grows, you'll need to hire more and more people who will inevitably lack your charisma, smarts, and depth of knowledge. If yours is like most growing organizations, you probably spend a large fortune recruiting, hiring, and training new employees. For their training alone, you can make up much of the gap through superior systems that enable faster sharing of institutional knowledge. Many of the founders I know sell by sheer force of their personality, their unique knowledge base, and their inherent people skills. The only way to transfer some percentage of those capacities to hired-gun salespeople is through a strong company culture that includes proper training and institutional support. There is no alternative if you truly want to scale the company.

THIS MEANS YOU, TOO!

If you are a founder with highly developed technical skills, it's equally important for you to record and document your technical processes. Detailed comments in your code, documentation, release notes, and use cases may take time away from moving ahead with new innovations, but again, you must slow down to speed up. Knowledge recorded and stored (and readily retrievable) gives you the potential to transfer, train for, and leverage that knowledge for years to come, making your company's knowledge database a uniquely valuable asset. Great systems and processes beget great value. If it's all in your head, it's not worth much to your successor, or to anyone else.

Someday, perhaps someday soon, you are going to want to either raise capital or bring about a liquidity event. The value of your company very much depends upon the quality of your systems, documentation, and institutional knowledge. Without these systems in place, you may be building a great company, but not one that anyone will want to buy. That's the risk a company faces when the company's storehouse of knowledge is scattered around or stored only in the founder's head. Investors will want a deep discount for taking on the risk of that storehouse of knowledge walking out the door one day—or potentially getting hit by a bus.

Think about how establishing these institutional systems

strengthens The Founder Value Ladder and ensures that they can hold the weight of both you and future leaders to come.

"In the grand scheme of things, this won't make any difference."

Inevitably, despite all the processes and procedures that have been set up, founders will get involved in making deals. Big deals, you might rationalize, require your personal attention. So if you must get involved with deal making, certain boundaries are absolutely necessary to protect yourself and your company.

I have two important rules for founders who are directly involved in customer deals:

1. Never quote a price.

2. Never promise a specific delivery date.

These rules evolved after surviving a number of terrible experiences with deal-horny founders. I worked with one founder who was great at closing deals, but over time I realized that the reason he closed so many sales was because he was a pushover for client demands. Later I'd find our teams jumping through ridiculous, unnatural hoops at great expense, just to deliver what the founder had promised within unrealistically tight time frames. Then, when I examined the details of these lousy contracts, I found that he had also left a lot of money on the table, often unnecessarily.

Over time, I got increasingly nervous every time the founder closed a new deal, wondering what fresh hell he'd cooked up for us this time. Finally, I set these two rules, so he could use his unique talents to advance a deal with a client to a certain point—but when it came to pricing and delivery, he was *required* to consult with others more objective about what it would take to actually make money on the deal.

I've run into this problem in almost every business I've been involved in. The founder agrees to a difficult deliverable, one that will demand nothing less than superhuman efforts from the product team. The founder is delighted about all the new revenue he's generated and the important new customer, oblivious to how many ways he has cost his company time and money, plus the incalculable cost of alienating the product and delivery teams. (Sometimes the founder's *need* to make deals can blindside the legal team, as well.) Then he gets frustrated when the team finds it difficult to live up to the expectations he set.

Customers ask founders for discounts because they know founders have a hard time saying "no." Some founders don't want to appear weak by admitting they can't close the deal on their own, but it's completely reasonable to say, "I'm going to have to check with my team and see what we can do. They'll be able to give us some options on how we can meet that deadline with those requirements." And your team will be able to do that, if you give them the chance. If you tell your team a customer needs a discount or an expedited delivery, at least allow them to consider the request and tell you what's achievable. Don't make that commitment to the customer and come back to the office with new, unrealistic marching orders.

It's much more advantageous to hand off deal closing to your sales staff; it makes the final negotiations much easier to handle, as well.

"It's much more advantageous to hand off deal closing to your sales staff; it makes the final negotiations much easier to handle, as well."

If the customer springs a trap, or an unusual request, the salesperson can defer to his absent boss and avoid making the decision in the moment. You recognize this from having negotiated to purchase a car, when the salesperson has to consult with his sales manager, who never seems to be available in person. There is, however, a difference between a salesperson who says "yes" and the same answer from his boss. The boss can always reverse the salesperson's decision by explaining that the salesperson never had the appropriate authority. However, a founder has a much harder time saying "yes" at the table and then walking it back later.

THE BIGGER YOU ARE, THE HARDER YOU FALL

Making early sales and growing revenue is critical to the validation of any startup company. Sometimes its very survival depends on the founder agreeing to do the impossible—the way Bill Gates legendarily put tiny Microsoft's future on the line by agreeing to deliver IBM's first PC operating system against an unrealistic deadline, while not having a clear plan for how this would happen (or even where he would get such an operating system—since Microsoft didn't have one at the time). Founders live and die by their early sales success, which is why sales can become like a drug addiction to the founder. As your company grows, you need to be prevented from hurting the company through your deal making. Not that you would do that purposely. But with the authority to do whatever it takes to make the sale, founders can maneuver through objections like a slalom course. The addiction to sales means the founder can and will do almost anything to make the sale.

While a founder's deal navigation skills may be required in the early days, remember that the bigger you get, the harder you fall. As the company grows and matures, you're playing for higher stakes, which means even minor errors in seat-of-the-pants deal making can have much larger consequences than you can imagine.

"As the company grows and matures, you're playing for higher stakes, which means even minor errors in seat-of-the-pants deal making can have much larger consequences than you can imagine."

That's the most important takeaway from this chapter. As your organization scales, it becomes ever more important to ensure that what you do is well documented and conforms to an objective standard that will serve the company for years to come. Documentation and process allows your team to leverage its collective knowledge and protect you from yourself and your craving for revenue.

Don't let the following happen to you. A startup founder was eager to make an important sale to a large, well-known company. Closing the deal would mean instant credibility for the startup, and several hundred thousand dollars of much-needed annual recurring revenue guaranteed for several years to come. In order to get the deal done, the founder agreed to the customer's request for the right to make an offer to acquire the startup should it come up for sale.

It seemed like an innocuous provision at the time, because the startup was far from being ready to be sold. This was only a right to make an *offer*, not a guaranteed right of purchase or even a *right of first refusal*. Clearly if someone else wanted to buy the company and was willing to pay more money, this provision wouldn't even come into play. In the grand scheme of things, this would be totally innocuous. Or would it?

Fast-forward ten years. The startup had grown into a sizeable operation, and a sale was being negotiated for many times the value of that customer contract. The purchase moved to the due diligence phase, when suddenly that customer's right to make an offer emerged like a ticking time bomb. The buyer suddenly got cold feet about the deal and threatened to walk away. Feeling a bit like a stalking horse, the buyer reckoned that all the time and effort they were about to expend putting together a deal could go to waste if this one big customer exercised its ten-year-old contractual right to make a slightly higher offer. And as it turned out, this customer was a competitor of the buyer. It was touch-and-go for a while, as they gingerly negotiated around the issue and finally closed the deal. Long, sleepless nights and a brush with disaster, all because of a seemingly harmless agreement made a decade earlier that shouldn't have mattered in the grander scheme.

FOUR

JUST ASK WHY

"I'm *OK* hiring someone as long as they don't slow me down."

When I joined Transcentive near the end of the 1990s, I knew that everyone in the software industry was worried about the impending "Y2K effect." All over the world, an estimated $500 billion was being spent on computer system upgrades to ensure that when the millennium arrived, computer code, wherever it might be found, would properly recognize that the year was 2000 and not 1900. So it was natural to ask Transcentive's head of engineering about the issue. He assured me that all our code had already been checked out and cleared as Y2K-compatible.

Then, perhaps because I was new, or perhaps because of my anal-retentive ways, I made a request that would end up saving the company millions of dollars (and quite possibly its good name within the industry). I asked the technical team to test-run the major functions of the software with the date artificially set at the year 2000. I wanted to see what would happen if the computer was fooled into behaving as though the first day of the new millennium had already passed.

The tech team grudgingly complied and, just as they had predicted, our newer line of products ran flawlessly. But our older, legacy products almost immediately started sorting dates incorrectly, generating a rapidly growing torrent of errors. Although few of our customers were still using these older products, several of those customers ranked among our largest and most important. If we had allowed these big, well-known companies to keep running our software on January 1, 2000, they would have spent the following days and weeks contending with a bewildering set of reports. I shudder to think what such a debacle would have cost us in broken relationships, negative online buzz, and damaging coverage in the trade press.

The test run also revealed a larger, organization-wide problem at Transcentive. A letter had been sent to all our customers months earlier, assuring them that our systems had been tested for Y2K compatibility. Evidently, no one at Transcentive had been absolutely certain that such a claim was true before that letter went out. So now we had more than a software problem. We had a credibility problem. We had to go back to some of our largest customers and explain that our previous letter had been in error, and now, with the year 2000 bearing down on them, the software they were running was unsound and in need of immediate attention.

A LITTLE PROCESS GOES A LONG WAY

In the previous chapter, I emphasized the importance of document-ing internal processes, policies, and procedures so that the company can scale without relying on the founder's decisions on every little thing. The truth is that most founders don't much like policies and procedures. Founders got where they are by following their inde-pendent judgment and getting everyone to pull in behind them with that same seat-of-the-pants approach to getting things done. It's a rare founder who appreciates how policies and procedures contrib-ute to building company value. More often, founders tend to react to any new rules and protocols as bureaucratic nonsense that intrudes on their freewheeling management style.

For all of these reasons, founders tend to avoid instituting work-place policies and procedures until long after they're needed. Usually it takes a truly dumb and costly mistake or a near-death experience like the one above to persuade them that it's time to run a tighter ship. And even then, once the new policies are in place, most found-ers will evade them personally and avoid enforcing them. At least until the next costly mistake.

The better alternative is to bring aboard a manager who has as much passion for policies and procedures as you have for avoiding them. You're a company founder because you think differently, and now it's time to think differently yet again. The stakes have grown, the game has changed, and winning at the new game requires adding a senior team member who has more managerial experience than you. Ideally, I'd prefer this to be a person who doesn't know your industry too well. That's not a typo. *Doesn't* is the correct term. I want someone who brings lots of experience and few preconceptions.

I want someone who won't be embarrassed to ask a lot of naïve, uncomfortable questions—like the one I asked about Y2K.

Scaling up requires you to keep changing your organization *before* you think the organization needs to change.

> "Scaling up requires you to keep changing your
> organization before you think the organization
> needs to change."

It obliges you to be reined in by the same policies and procedures that will raise the game for everyone on your team. A few rare founders can take charge of these changes on their own, but the smart ones bring in someone more experienced to lead the way.

Reid Hoffman was one of those founders who stepped up to the challenge. He made the decision that he was not the right guy to do this heavy lifting at LinkedIn and hired Dan Nye and then Jeff Weiner to scale the company. While Weiner was not the one who defined the culture at LinkedIn (Hoffman was), he was the guy who codified the culture in a way that made it understandable to the growing population of employees.

The alternative is that every day your company grows larger and more successful, it becomes a bit more difficult to hold The Founder Value Ladder steady. It also grows one day closer to a costly debacle that could end up bringing it down. It's very likely you've gotten this far by keeping everyone in your wake and out of your way, with a minimum of bureaucratic hassle. Now you need to recognize that company growth has a funny way of slowly transforming the management style you've cherished as your formula for success into a prescription for disaster.

"That's how we do it here."

On that day when I first raised the Y2K question at Transcentive, the head of engineering rolled his eyes and scoffed that I would even bother asking about it. Think about that. He was absolutely confident about a software product that proved to be so deeply flawed that it failed a fairly simple test run. Was he incompetent? Negligent? Of course not. He was a very smart and capable guy. But that's what goes wrong when smart, capable people at a fast-growing company make decisions in the absence of management controls that maintain accountability. With no set procedures for documenting software testing and no policies for reviewing draft letters before sending them to customers, it was inevitable that one day something big would fall through the cracks at Transcentive.

The test run revealed the problem with the software very quickly, but addressing that problem was neither quick nor easy. We discovered the issue so late, having already assured our customers that their software was fine, that we had to scramble to send out our prescribed remedies along with our humble apologies. Transcentive ended up offering most of the affected customers deeply discounted upgrades to the newer software. But because that software wasn't compatible with the outdated systems that some of our customers still relied upon, it wasn't an appropriate solution. For those customers, we had to rush in and help with time-consuming software code fixes as the clock ticked down to December 31, 1999. The entire ordeal was embarrassing and expensive, though ultimately much cheaper than the catastrophe we had narrowly avoided.

If I have a passion for process, policies, and procedures, it's simply because I've seen how easily companies can be badly damaged without them. I don't ask uncomfortable questions because I enjoy the bad feelings and occasional dirty looks such questions arouse. I ask because when people are called upon to look at the things they'd rather not look at, hidden value for the company frequently gets unlocked in the process.

> "When people are called upon to look at the things they'd rather not look at, hidden value for the company frequently gets unlocked in the process."

I can't explain why the Transcentive engineers failed to test their legacy software more thoroughly before allowing that letter to go out to customers. I do know, however, that it took a series of very awkward conversations in order to expose that breakdown in organizational process in the nick of time.

Sound management processes hold people accountable, and accountability naturally generates conflict—especially when it's initiated where it's been lacking. My first year at Force 3 was marked by the introduction of quarterly staff meetings that were often very contentious. Each department head was required to prepare a review of their department's recent performance and spell out their strategies for improvement. Rocky, the company founder, didn't enjoy these meetings at all. The conflict built into the meeting format made him extremely uncomfortable and he used to joke nervously, "These meetings are the most fun you can have with your clothes on."

But Rocky also recognized their value. Having his department heads prepare for these meetings was a reliable way to root out problems that had been festering inside the company for years. Like them or not, the meetings ended up generating many of the ideas that would become key to the company's subsequent improvement. For instance, when the CFO at one meeting recommended asking the banks to increase our line of credit, we took a hard look at our cash flow and discovered that we were often slow to generate invoices, and our invoices weren't always complete or correct. By merely tightening up our invoicing processes, we greatly improved the company's cash flow fundamentals, ensuring that in the future we could access the credit we'd need to accommodate our plans for growth.

And yes, the meetings were very stressful. Not all the department heads still had their jobs a year later. But it's like how you want the contractor that comes to your house to replace the siding to inspect the support beams for rot before he puts up the new siding. It's critically important to get past what appears on the surface and identify what lies beneath, at the risk of finding something awful. Nothing can change, and things can get much worse, if you avoid shining a light on areas in your company that may be moldering in the dark.

STEELING YOURSELF
FOR THE TASK AT HAND

What I'm describing is difficult work, and not everyone enjoys it. You probably have a more congenial, entrepreneurial leadership style that generates excitement about your company's future, bolsters team morale, and puts a check on self-doubt and paralysis by analysis. As the organization matures, however, your duties will tend to transform from cheerleading to strategy execution. When a company reaches a certain size, trumpeting the positives becomes less important than finding and fixing the negatives, because hidden problems that cause negligible damage at a small company can be fatal to a larger one. The bigger your company becomes, the higher The Founder Value Ladder grows and the further the fall.

"The bigger your company becomes, the higher The Founder Value Ladder grows and the further the fall."

By the time your company grows past the startup phase, you are probably getting frustrated with the mounting tide of mundane tasks required to scale the organization, the daunting height of what's to come, and the fear of releasing your grip on the bottom ladder rungs. Unless you are excited by the prospect of learning how to master these responsibilities, you should consider giving way to someone who is. When you peel back the CEO mystique, the role isn't very sexy at all. It requires hard, unforgiving work that involves relentlessly seeking the truth—and then fashioning effective responses to each truth that's revealed. Some entrepreneurs discover that they enjoy the daily grind that's demanded of the CEO, but many more find the experience draining, if not debilitating.

SOME FOUNDERS AREN'T CUT OUT TO BE CEOS, AND THAT'S OK

Venture capitalist Mark Suster is one company founder who came to realize that the CEO role was not for him. "The truth is," he wrote in his blog, "I have never enjoyed running team meetings, managing processes [and] procedures and deciding HR policies, promotions and organizational structures."

After six years at one company he'd founded, he found himself in a rut where he "felt I had lost the ability to be innovative and . . . lost a bit of the passion and fun that came with the early days."

Without this level of insight and self-knowledge, many founders have a tendency to trap themselves in the CEO role and then do the job poorly. They are certain they know what works, so they rely on their strengths and ignore their weaknesses. Then their teams pull in behind them in lockstep, because follow-the-leader has always been the company's prime directive. At every level within the company, you can have people working harder than ever doing things the way that's always worked for them, with few people recognizing that the demands of scale are making the old ways increasingly ineffective, if not downright dangerous. For some companies, it amounts to a lemming-like march off a ledge.

The odd thing about this self-destructive organizational pattern is that it stems from programming code running inside every human brain. We prefer doing things the way we always have because our brains crave repetition. When Mark Suster felt he was in a rut, he was using an apt metaphor. Our brains create neural pathways, figurative "ruts" in the thought process, that lead us to repeat actions that have been successful and satisfying in the past. The trouble comes when circumstances change gradually but significantly—like when a company grows from a startup to a scalable business. Once we've been conditioned to assess and respond to problems in the same way we always have, we lose our ability to recognize new challenges for what they are, and to formulate responses with fresh thinking.

"Once we've been conditioned to assess and respond to problems in the same way we always have, we lose our ability to recognize new challenges for what they are, and to formulate responses with fresh thinking."

Social scientists call this quirk in thinking "The Curse of Knowledge." We have a cognitive bias in which deep expertise both sharpens and narrows our vision. It's as though we develop 20/10 acuity with blinders on. The Curse of Knowledge generates ineffectiveness and failure because it discourages us from understanding subtle changes in our circumstances. Like the frog in the boiling pot, the warming water feels just fine until it's too late. We continue to follow the trodden path, because the more we know, the more we enjoy knowing what we know—and the more we dislike and mistrust our feelings of ignorance and doubt. Thanks to The Curse of Knowledge, we will make assumptions and leap to conclusions that we would normally treat with more skepticism, if only we knew less!

Experiments in cognitive biases related to The Curse of Knowledge reveal how expertise in solving one specific type of problem blinds you to opportunities for new learning and understanding. Test subjects were given a series of maze problems to solve, all of which had very similar solutions. Then they were given a maze problem that looked a lot like the others, but also contained some critical shortcuts that the others lacked. When these test subjects participated in timed sessions, almost all of them failed to see the shortcuts in the final maze. Even though they were offered cash rewards for solving the final maze quickly, they followed the same kind of time-consuming roundabout approach they had learned from doing the previous puzzles. On the other hand, another group of test subjects who were given just the final maze without being exposed to the earlier ones recognized those shortcuts almost immediately. Test subjects with "less expertise" in solving puzzles were better at solving the final puzzle.

Effects of these kinds are pervasive in fast-growing companies. Every day brings new challenges that employees attack by applying yesterday's intuitions and methods. Year-over-year sales increases convince us how smart we are, yet operations may be needlessly slow because experienced people can't see more efficient alternatives staring them in the face. The pot is beginning to boil, but all we feel is the soothing warm water.

This is where structures for process and accountability can save the day. Expertise is valuable, and it's impossible to take on every new task with a commitment to see it anew. But systems and structures can be put in place to prompt questioning (such as "How do we know this letter to our customers is correct?"). They can provoke productive self-doubt and introspection where the natural human proclivity is to avoid complications and instead do whatever feels right and familiar.

"I'm not sure you understand how different this company is."

Almost all the founders I've met have assured me in one way or another that their business is very special and much more complex than I can imagine. Every founder I've worked for has similarly expressed a serious concern that my lack of specific industry expertise was a serious disadvantage to my ability to make a positive impact. One told me with great confidence that nothing I had learned from my other business experiences would apply at his company. Another insisted that I could not be effective in helping his company unless he first taught me everything he knew about the industry.

You likely have similar sentiments about your company, and you're probably correct that your business is very complex. Most businesses are. Otherwise, everyone would be a founder. However, beliefs of this kind can also have the negative effect of building a protective wall around The Curse of Knowledge. I'm willing to accept that you know more than me about your company and your industry, but if you use that superior knowledge to avoid my questions or dispute what I've discovered, then we are both on a dangerous path.

"You just don't understand the nuances of our business" is never an acceptable answer to a question about why things are or aren't done a certain way. In fact, whenever I hear someone invoking their superior knowledge or expertise to avoid explaining themselves clearly, I feel certain that I've run across a very big problem that needs fixing.

"Whenever I hear someone invoking their superior knowledge or expertise to avoid explaining themselves clearly, I feel certain that I've run across a very big problem that needs fixing."

I'm a little like Al Pacino's character in the movie *The Insider*, where he plays a *60 Minutes* producer getting the runaround on a story about the tobacco industry. Pacino finally explodes at one point, "I'm gettin' pissed off and I'm gettin' curious!"

LOOK BEYOND REVENUE GROWTH

When I arrived at Force 3, Rocky suggested to me that his business was the most complex I had ever been involved with. It's true that his business of reselling network hardware to federal agencies required a thorough knowledge of arcane procurement rules—rules I had never encountered and had no real interest in learning. Most of my background up until then involved commercial markets and software with very different procurement processes and significantly higher gross margins than the resale of computer equipment. On the other hand, I understood some basics about how to succeed in the highly competitive reseller game and, perhaps most important, wasn't afraid to ask naïve questions. Force 3 had no proprietary products, and therefore, like any other high-volume commodity operation, the key indicator for profitability would be gross margin. All funding for overhead and profits are drawn from the difference between the selling price and the cost of delivery, so the daily objective in any commodity business is to reduce overhead costs and grow gross margins.

The company was just getting by on the slimmest of margins at the time, and I was brought on partly because Rocky understood that the slightest nudge in the wrong direction could bring the whole company down. I assumed that everyone understood the importance of generating the largest possible margin on each new sale, because it was clear to me that the company's survival depended on it. Nonetheless, I decided to ask the sales management team some deliberately naïve questions about margins. To my astonishment, they agreed on one thing: margin percentages didn't matter! As they saw it, there really was no difference at all between one revenue dollar at 2 percent gross margin and one revenue dollar at 15 percent gross margin. What mattered, they explained, was bringing in as many of those dollars as possible. I guessed they thought we would make it up in volume, and perhaps we were, at least up until that point.

On the one hand, their response struck me as absolutely outrageous. On the other, once I looked at how the sales force was compensated, I found it perfectly understandable. Commissions and bonuses at Force 3 were pegged solely on dollars of margin, with no regard for the margin's percentage. Salespeople naturally avoided the more difficult long sales cycles required to sell high-margin products because the big-revenue low-margin deals were quicker and easier.

How could this happen? The short answer is that revenue growth is very seductive. Revenue is all too often the measure of your company's importance, your impact on your industry, and your personal status as a founder. Revenue growth gets you on the *Inc.* 500 list. In the reseller business in particular, the larger your annual revenue, the more attention you garner from your large manufacturer partners. This helps explain the revenue-driven sales culture at Force 3. Getting bigger helped the company's notoriety and enabled Rocky to get his calls returned from his suppliers. Their cooperation and attention was essential to Force 3's ability to deliver the goods. This was critically important to the company's success. But at some point, revenue growth can become an unhealthy addiction. If you continue to maintain your chief focus on revenue growth, your company will risk growing itself out of business.

The fix at Force 3 was simple enough. Overnight, we changed sales incentives so that the lowest-margin sales earned no commission. From there, commission rates scaled upward to correspond with margin percentages. It took only a few months under this new compensation schedule before gross margins improved by more than one full point. Multiplied by several hundred million in revenues, that one-percentage-point increase made a substantial difference in operating income and profits that year. Best of all, I had managed to help improve our balance sheet without having to first become an expert in the complex rules of government procurement.

Most of us are unwilling to ask dumb questions because we don't want others to think we're stupid or naïve. To me, however, there is no better way to ferret out the reality of a situation than by asking a series of dumb questions.

"There is no better way to ferret out the reality of a situation than by asking a series of dumb questions."

Sometimes I ask them because I truly don't know any better. But sometimes I know the answer and I need to know if the people around me are on the same page. There is a line from one of Steve Jobs's favorite books, *Zen Mind, Beginner's Mind*: "In the beginner's mind there are many possibilities, but in the expert's mind there are few."

Asking questions as though I am an ignorant beginner is how I'm able to test the possibilities of a given situation.

Whenever I think about the effectiveness of naïve questions, I recall the television detective show *Columbo* from the late 1960s and 1970s. Peter Falk played Columbo, a homicide detective with the Los Angeles Police Department, a bumbling, disheveled detective who was consistently underestimated by his suspects. He used his apparent absentmindedness and unassuming appearance as a shrewd tool to solve his cases.

On numerous occasions, I've interrupted a conversation to ask someone to explain the meaning of what they've just said. Usually I find out much more about what they know, but on occasion I've learned that someone doesn't truly know what he's talking about—he's parroting received knowledge. It's way too easy to let vague, authoritative-sounding statements slip by, and to take whatever the contents of the statement are as the truth, without raising questions that would have been asked by Columbo.

On other occasions I've asked for clarification, only to discover that no one else knows the answer either. I can recall one early meeting at a company, where a three-letter acronym used by the federal government was used over and over again until I paused the meeting to ask what those letters stood for. Despite the fact that three or four of the attendees in the meeting had more than two decades each of experience working with the government, not a person in the room could answer my question.

This could explain what appeared to me to be an odd quirk of one of my former board members—Harry Gruner. Harry, a founding partner with the private equity firm JMI, had arguably good auditory function but would often ask me to repeat an answer I had given him. It wasn't because he hadn't heard my answer. Instead, it was his way to get me to expand my explanations beyond what he viewed as my formerly vague response. Unfortunately, it took me until now to realize this.

As best as you can, you must try to see things yourself from the perspective of a beginner, because your expertise always threatens to block your view of the truth about what's going on in your company.

"You must try to see things yourself from the perspective of a beginner, because your expertise always threatens to block your view of the truth about what's going on in your company."

If your next hire is someone who can bring an outsider's questioning perspective to the management of the organization, so much the better. When you hear team members say things like "This is the way we've always done it," or "We tried that and it didn't work," you should understand that if those patterns of thinking go unchallenged and unquestioned, your organization will be doomed to relive its past while missing opportunities to seize the future.

"That would mean giving up a key advantage."

In theory it shouldn't be very difficult to steer a company toward larger-margin products that are scalable and sustainable. In practice, however, your team may be emotionally invested in lower-margin products, because it took a low-margin approach to drive your early revenue growth. A move toward higher margins can appear to be a high-risk strategy that threatens competitive advantage—although in truth there are few activities that carry a higher risk than growing ever larger on low-margin sales—unless you have built the cost efficiencies of a WalMart.

At Transcentive, for instance, Mike Brody, its founder, ingeniously figured out early on how to generate sales by offering his most demanding customers highly flexible and customizable software products. Transcentive was willing to make whatever software modifications the customer desired, and the company very effectively built market share by using this product differentiation to outflank larger competitors and their one-size-fits-all offerings. This kind of personalized customer service is a common niche approach for any startup trying to crack a market dominated by big players. For Transcentive, customization was a point of differentiation that they were proud of and came to rely on.

But customization was a potentially deadly Achilles heel in the company's efforts to scale. Constantly modified software is difficult to service, and demands for that service are chunky and unpredictable, which hampers the ability to forecast and manage growth. What was worse, the margins on customized software were much lower than those of packaged software. When you sell packaged software, the work you do for each customer is applicable to all the others. But with the bespoke software they were creating, they would not get that kind of leverage and couldn't charge those customers nearly enough to generate similar profits. The more they sold, the larger the burden on their infrastructure.

I had the opportunity to join Transcentive around then and recommended we modify the pitch deck by removing the slide on customizable software. Mike reacted as though I had uttered an unfathomable heresy. Mike and customization were attached like Linus and his security blanket. He understood very well that customization is the strategic opposite of scalability—labor intensive, unpredictable, and margin eroding. But he feared that without the customizing features, our sales would suffer. Nonetheless, and to Mike's credit, he went along with my plan, knowing it was my throat he would choke if this failed.

In a sense, The Curse of Knowledge had Mike under its spell. Customization had secured his young company its first strategic beachhead, and what Mike hadn't recognized was that over time, that beachhead no longer needed defending. Transcentive products had gained new competitive advantages as the company had grown. Selling points for the software now included its reputation for quality, the credibility of broker partners, and its significant market position. Contrary to Mike's fears, after the company pulled back from customization, the following several years saw extremely strong annual sales growth in its highest-margin products. None of those products carried the burdensome service commitments that Mike and the rest of the company had only recently regarded as absolutely essential to sales growth.

HERESY IS MAGIC

There is magic to heresy, and it's healthy to have some heretics around, as long as they're not obnoxious about it (which is a very important point I had to learn the hard way). You want people on your team who aren't afraid to cast doubt on the value of sacred cows, especially your low-margin "cash cows" that generate lots of revenue and lots of headaches. The benefits can be so great that a culture of questioning in the business can become contagious—a culture that is fraught with the curiosity to ask *Why?* You really want your top people to be comfortable with doubt—comfortable enough to f**k things up and then fix them.

> *"You really want your top people to be comfortable with doubt—comfortable enough to f**k things up and then fix them."*

As a general principle, there's something to be said for seeking people with diverse backgrounds, because they can also bring that quality of questioning to the company. In a wonderful book called *The Medici Effect*, Frans Johansson discusses how innovation and breakthrough thinking can occur at the intersection of unrelated disciplines. Attracting a diverse set of people with backgrounds in unrelated disciplines can be just the ingredients for your future growth. Leveraging their diverse experiences, making mistakes in those different environments, learning from those mistakes, and piecing together a pattern from the tapestry of various incidents can be just what your business needs.

The downside for you is that over a period of time, you might begin to feel that the company you've nurtured from nothing will begin to look and feel unrecognizable to you. Changes in focus might even create some "J-curve" effects in which things get worse before they get better. In the short term, it may look like things are going off the rails, when really you've taken a half step backward in order to leap forward. As a metaphor, consider how a snake must shed its outer skin in order to grow. In certain stages of the skin-shedding process, a molting snake is an awful sight. But just the opposite is occurring. If you've never seen it before, you might assume the snake is injured and dying. In fact, molting is a sign of robust health in a snake, as it is in all animals that shed their skins. Molting indicates that the animal is so well nourished that it needs a new skin to accommodate its increasing bulk.

A CULTURE OF QUESTIONS

I'm convinced the future belongs to companies that are good at asking questions. One reason is that superior knowledge is no longer a strong source of competitive advantage. Accessing knowledge is now so easy to do, and there's so much information freely available, that knowing lots of stuff doesn't give you the edge it once did, except perhaps on *Jeopardy*. According to Kevin Kelly, the founding executive editor of *Wired* magazine, "In the world that Google is constructing—a world of cheap and free answers—having answers isn't going to be very significant or important. Having a really great question will be where the value is."

Amid this glut of information, the more important attribute for a company is a culture that supports questioning, curiosity, and inquiry. By asking lots of questions, and pursuing the truth with dogged determination, you stand a better chance of hitting on solutions that will derive meaning and create value from the vast amounts of knowledge now at everyone's fingertips.

Questions, more than answers, unlock potential that goes far beyond the status quo.

"Questions, more than answers, unlock potential that goes far beyond the status quo."

According to Warren Berger, the author of the best-selling book *A More Beautiful Question*, "questions are the foundation for innovation." He writes:

> "Why can't it be done that way? Why not add this? Why would someone do that? And, questions like: 'Wouldn't it be cool if . . .' have formed the foundation of some of the world's greatest startups."

Inevitably, you want this questioning culture to develop as the next phase to replace your startup culture, which is largely the cult of you as the founder. A culture of questioning, led perhaps by an experienced professional inserted as your COO or even your CEO, is how you secure the health of your company if it should ever need to run without you—for a month, for a year, or maybe forever. What if tomorrow you came down with a debilitating illness or were in a serious accident? What if you died? If, like most founders, you have nearly all your personal wealth wrapped up in the company you founded, shouldn't you be sure that if something happens to you, you're leaving behind a management team and a culture that can allow your family to reap the benefits of all of your hard work?

We're all mortal, and none of us are guaranteed another day. You might enjoy your freewheeling management style, but it's important to have something more durable in place in case the unexpected happens. Keep in mind that your people can't just follow your lead and stay in your wake if they happen to have just attended your wake!

FIVE

THE EMPEROR HAS NO CLOTHES

"I will never consider removing one of our founding team members."

Back in 1999, before he was a well-known leadership guru, Ram Charan wrote in *Fortune* magazine that his study of failed CEOs revealed one fatal shortcoming most of them shared: failure to execute by their direct reports. Almost two decades later, the lesson still resonates and is particularly applicable to founder CEOs.

"So how do CEOs blow it?" Charan wrote with co-author Geoffrey Colvin. "More than any other way, by failure to put the right people in the right jobs—and the related failure to fix people problems in time."

The root problem cited in the article was a failure of emotional strength when it came to holding subordinates accountable. When you fail to fire people who aren't getting the job done—*you* fail. The company fails, too.

"When you fail to fire people who aren't getting the job done—you fail."

"Failed CEOs are often unable to deal with a few key subordinates whose sustained poor performance deeply harms the company," Charan and Colvin continued. "What is striking, as many CEOs told us, is that they usually know there's a problem; their inner voice is telling them, but they suppress it. Those around the CEO often recognize the problem first, but he isn't seeking information from multiple sources. As one CEO says, 'It was staring me in the face, but I refused to see it.'"

It's likely that as a founder you love your team but worry about whether your vision, your strategy, or your read of the markets is leading your team in the right direction. The truth is that lots of people have collaborated with you on your strategic decisions, and the collaboration has improved your chances of being right. But people decisions are very personal to you, the founder. These personnel decisions, which to keep and who to let go, are yours and yours alone. Lonely individual decisions rarely get exposed to contrary points of view. So it shouldn't be surprising that it is in this one particular area, which is at the leader's more-or-less complete discretion, where failed founder CEOs make their fatal errors.

DON'T MISTAKE LOYALTY FOR COMPETENCE

I've heard founders comment proudly that a loyal long-term subordinate is preferable to a more talented, more accomplished outsider who might not buy fully into the founder's vision. Founders fool themselves into thinking that loyalty is a type of competency that can't be found among outsiders. Instead, they might consider they are being told only what they want to hear. The truth is that founders who fail to upgrade personnel run into the exact problems that Ram Charan detected.

A subordinate can appear just as loyal as ever as the company scales. He might even go out of his way to appear more loyal than ever, just to remind the founder of his dedication and commitment—in the face of poor results.

Getting fooled by loyalty parading as competence is about as dangerous a condition as there is. All CEOs fall prey to the loyalty trap, but founders are particularly prone to misplaced loyalty because in the earliest days of entrepreneurial battle, when you are struggling to survive, uniformity of opinion equals uniformity of purpose. Loyalty is a prized quality because staying together, keeping the faith, and riding out the bumps is all that matters.

But the early value of loyalty fades as companies grow and the challenges change. I've often been known to state the always-unpopular axiom that if the composition of your executive team was right at $10 million of revenue, then they clearly are wrong at $50 million (and vice versa).

"If the composition of your executive team was right at $10 million of revenue, then they clearly are wrong at $50 million."

And while I implicitly believe this to be true, it doesn't mean that any of them are bad. It just means that the game has changed. Like the major league baseball prospect who hits .300 in AA ball but just can't hit the curve ball in the majors, this new level for the company is quite different and requires new and improved skills. Some, but not all, executives will learn to hit the breaking ball and improve their skills sufficiently to contribute at this level. But most will not. Your willingness to replace executives is a natural consequence of growth, and you are just going to have to be OK with that.

As the company grows and matures, however, there are more decisions to be made that require professionalism, expertise, and discernment. Your team creates company value at advanced stages of growth by asking hard questions and encouraging change—two things your loyal subordinates are least likely to do. You need to resist that temptation to reward past loyalty with misplaced confidence in subordinates who are not up to the task of helping you fight this next, larger battle. That requires you to gain the "emotional strength" that Ram Charan found lacking in so many failed CEOs.

"People are always candid with me."

I remember vividly the first day I spent in an executive-titled role. It was at Progress Software, a public software company in the Boston area, and Greg O'Connor, then a member of the technical team and now an accomplished founder and CEO, entered my office and shut the door behind me. Although we certainly didn't yet know each other very well, he had an important thought to share with me:

"From this day forward," he said, "no employee of this company will ever tell you the truth."

At the time, I wondered if Greg was trying to warn me about a particularly toxic cultural issue at our company, but now I know better. It's true for every executive. The more power you hold, the more reluctant your employees are to level with you.

"The more power you hold, the more reluctant your employees are to level with you."

People in authority attract rose-colored versions of reality all day long, and if you're not sufficiently skeptical about what you hear, you can easily find yourself in trouble.

To avoid falling prey to hearing what people think you would like to hear, you've got to be willing to accept that not everything you hear will be complimentary. The truth, it turns out, is often ugly, unfortunate, and embarrassing. To a founder who is used to all the positive energy and optimism that it takes to launch a new company, the awful truth can sound a lot like negativity and defeatism. But it's not. The truth is what you need to hear if you want to make decisions that are fully informed. After all, there is one thing worse than being told you have a booger hanging from your nose. Not being told!

BEING HUMAN

So how can a founder create an environment that invites truth-telling and frank discussions of the issues at hand?

1. Try to keep your ego under wraps so that people aren't afraid to tell you the truth

I have a healthy degree of self-confidence, but I've also found that the best way to avoid the appearance of being egotistical is to deliberately create opportunities to appear vulnerable, to be human, warts and all. For me, inviting an employee to play golf is close to perfect. Unless you maintain a single-digit handicap, golf is a humbling game. When I am golfing, I am far from perfect and the ugly reality of my golf game breaks down barriers that might ordinarily obstruct the truth. But by appearing vulnerable, or perhaps even just human, your employees will be more apt to trust that you are like them. Anything you can do to open yourself up in this way will make it easier for your employees to point out a weakness, identify a failure, or just state a contrary opinion that you need to know about.

2. Proactively invite feedback within this open environment

In the previous chapter, I discussed the importance of asking questions. Shake the trees and see what fruit falls out of them. I'm not talking about using the third degree in your questioning; just being curious will be sufficient to evidence your empathy. You must never forget that as the company grows, it's what you don't know that poses the greatest threat to your success.

3. Embrace the feedback when it's received

No one really likes feedback unless it's a hundred percent positive, so you need to adjust your attitude. One view is to try to regard difficult feedback as a valuable gift: if it's hard for you to hear, then it was probably harder for the bearer to deliver it, and the reason the individual went to that trouble is probably because the piece of feedback is important. Try to assume that the more it hurts, the more value it might hold. And be sure to thank them, no matter how difficult it may be for you to accept.

4. Once you've accepted the feedback gracefully, you should be prepared to do something with it

This point relates to a fundamental fact about workplace engagement and satisfaction. Companies that study these issues say that you should never survey your employees unless you're prepared to acknowledge the results and make changes based on them. The same goes for inviting feedback from your employees. You can't put up the pretense of being open to comments and criticism unless you're willing to follow through and follow up in some substantive way. That's how you keep the channels of communication open.

During my career I set these four steps in motion by holding regularly scheduled town meetings. The meetings were intended to be casual, animated, and fun, often including some adult refreshments (which in moderation can be an effective facilitator of the truth). I often began the meeting with a story in which I was the butt of the joke, usually about how I had screwed something up in my professional past. Other times I'd share personal anecdotes, like how in high school I had longer hair than my classmate Dee Snider, who went on to lead the heavy metal band Twisted Sister, all of which was intended to demonstrate the safety of this forum. That was usually all it took to start up a flow of productive comments and questions.

I also held impromptu "lunches with Les" with small groups that were working on a critical project or with a department that was under some stress. Taking people outside the office, without an agenda, to chat over a pizza or Chinese food is a nice informal way to get people to share their thoughts and concerns. Who said there is no free lunch?

In all of these encounters, I make very sure that when someone volunteers an important tidbit of truth, I restate it to make sure it's properly understood and heard by all, and then take a moment to thank the contributor. Later, when I subsequently take action on that piece of feedback, I make sure to acknowledge that person publicly in some way, either at a later group meeting or through a group email. I also follow up with a personal note of thanks and, if at all possible, indicate the specific positive results of their contribution.

I want to make sure everyone knows that I am not the kind of boss that shoots the messenger. The truth may sometimes be painful, but it is precious, and I try to treat it that way.

AVOID ANONYMOUS FEEDBACK

Over the years, I've had requests to accept anonymous feedback. My personal opinion is that this locked "suggestion box" approach to fixing problems ultimately carries too much risk of backfiring. Yes, there may be some facts that are so embarrassing or damaging that you need to know them right away, and allowing the source his or her anonymity is a fair price to pay. The trouble is that whenever you act on an anonymous tip, you can't really be sure of what you're getting into, and ultimately you're not helping build a culture of truthfulness. If feedback without attribution is allowed to have an impact, what message does that send about transparency and honesty in the workplace?

"If feedback without attribution is allowed to have an impact, what message does that send about transparency and honesty in the workplace?"

On the other hand, you can't let the company suffer just because some people are reluctant to be fully forthcoming. So one solution

I've found for this particular problem is to create a committee of thought leaders across departments of the company whose job it is to pick up thoughts that people might be afraid to express openly. The committee members are people I feel are particularly honest, enjoy good relationships among their team members, and have a decent grip on the realities facing the company—all our faults and flaws.

Then I ask the members of this group to come to me with the "anonymous" feedback for us to discuss and consider, but I also ask that they not represent any idea unless they too are convinced it's an honest and relevant concern. In that way, at least one named person (among the members of this committee) is personally responsible for the feedback. We would meet several times a year and ramble through issues they felt were most important. And I got what I asked for. In several situations I was overwhelmed by the magnitude and honesty of their suggestions. I was truly surprised by some of the suggestions. In one case, we had considered paying sales commissions earlier—at the time the sale was concluded—rather than waiting until we were paid by the customer. I heard overwhelming opposition to this idea, even though it appeared to be in the sales-people's interest. It turned out, they would rather be certain of their commission and know that it might not later be reversed than be paid earlier, a result I never would have expected.

YOU NEED A HEARING AID

For all these efforts, the facts that come to your attention will none-theless still be spotty and diluted by the time they reach you. That's where your next-in-command can help. Finding a trusted num-ber-two who has an ear to the ground and a clear line of sight to the truth is an invaluable asset for any leader. You need one person who will tell you when the emperor has no clothes—or has a booger hanging from his nose.

The cautionary note here is that if you do indeed find such a person willing to feed you the unvarnished truth, you need to embrace that feedback and work with that person to implement a response. Their feedback is a gift that must be coveted. If it's not, if you shrug it off, if you cast it away, your next-in-command will become a yes-man or yes-woman—a soothsayer to calm your nerves as all around you goes to pieces.

The truth may hurt, but white lies and sugarcoated half-truths will kill you.

"The truth may hurt, but white lies and sugarcoated half-truths will kill you."

You don't have the time to bask in fairy tales in which your team will indulge you. You need to overstate your intention to be told the unvarnished truth about just about everything, and you must find tangible ways to reward and publicly acknowledge every messenger willing to deliver you a dose of reality. All this effort in truth-seeking is necessary because without it, the default mode for your employees will be to hide the truth from you for fear of displeasing you. And once that ethos becomes ingrained in your company culture, disaster is always lurking right around the corner.

A friend who is the COO at a California-based startup received a text message very early one morning from his new financial controller, who asked to meet with him first thing that morning. When he got to the office, the controller sheepishly entered the COO's office and closed the door. "I've never done this before," he began. "But it looks like my boss (the CFO) is cooking the books." It was apparent to him that she had accrued revenue for this quarter that hadn't yet been booked, and she moved some current expenses out to the next quarter.

The founder of the company was vacationing in Europe. Could it be that the founder had told her to cook the books and file an untruthful quarterly statement? He knew the founder as someone with great integrity, but he also knew that weak numbers made the founder very irritable. In the past he'd heard the founder respond to a disappointing quarterly report by grumbling how "that can't be right," and instructing the CFO to double-check the math. Could it be that the founder had actually instructed the CFO to manipulate the numbers to conform to his wishes?

When the COO confronted the CFO, she admitted that the books were not really an accurate portrayal of the company's performance. She had indeed moved some expenses forward and booked some revenue that had not yet been received. She also assured him that the founder had never told her or even suggested that she bend the numbers in this way.

"Then why did you do this?" the exasperated COO finally asked.

"Because I wanted to make the founder happy!" she replied.

She said it as if it were common knowledge that making the founder happy was the prime directive for every employee at the company.

You may not realize it, but your innocent comments can have that kind of impact that can border on the illegal. So be careful with your words and do whatever is necessary to overstate your desire for the truth rather than being told what you would prefer.

"Our team is so close they can read each others' minds."

While visiting a Denver-based technology company several years ago, I was introduced to the executive vice president of administration, who told me he was responsible for the company's office space and equipment needs. I was curious how a small organization, with just a few hundred employees, could afford to carry an executive-level employee with such a limited role, so I asked the founder about it several hours later. "Oh, he's been a loyal supporter of the company from the day he joined," the founder explained. "He's not really capable of doing much more beyond his current duties, but I would never consider letting him go."

You might have similar people in your own organization. They may in fact be great team players, cheerleaders, and loyal followers, and you may value them for that. But if you knew the truth of how such people are viewed by their colleagues and how keeping them around impacts the expectations of your high performers, you might think very differently. When you heavily weigh down your executive ranks with people who are loyal but not competent for their current roles, the word gets out fast that your organization values "who you know" over what you can do.

> *"When you heavily weigh down your executive ranks with people who are loyal but not competent for their current roles, the word gets out fast that your organization values 'who you know' over what you can do."*

Those who don't penetrate the loyal core crowd will assume that their path to promotion is blocked, despite their value to the company. What results is rampant turnover, predominantly among your most talented new hires.

Common wisdom says that strong social ties among team members create a happier and more productive workforce. But according to a 2014 study, too much team camaraderie can actually backfire. I've seen founding teams that are together for a substantial period of time become insular, expecting that they know more than they do. Team dynamics can establish barriers to outsiders and promote a lack of interest in new ideas, and without injections of fresh thinking, their knowledge can become stale and their processes ritualistic, unresponsive to changes in the market—a "not invented here" mentality—believing that if they didn't invent something themselves, it must not be any good.

I once attended a meeting at a company going through such a transition, where everyone in the meeting was presented with an impressive thirty-page report filled with color-coded annotated numbers in rows and columns. Before I knew it, we were deep into a discussion of the report's details. People were commenting, the founder was opining, and heads were nodding, but I became increasingly confused. I couldn't tell which numbers were positive indicators, and which ones were negative. When I asked, the team couldn't agree on the meaning of the numbers either. As with many ingrained cultures I've encountered, the quantity of data was more important than the quality. These meetings were part of a ritual in which the longtime team members all showed up to impress each other with so much data that they had an answer for every question. No one, however, including the founder, was ready to decide amid

all that data which numbers mattered most—a management charac-
teristic that very nearly killed the company not long after.

CAUTION: FAST GROWTH AHEAD

Historically, fast growth is another danger sign that your company's scale now exceeds its executives' capabilities. In general, if your
company has grown by an order of magnitude (10x) from the time
a particular executive was hired, there is a pretty good chance that
this executive will not have the talent and ability necessary to help
you grow to the next order of magnitude. Certainly there are some
individuals who can scale their personal capabilities at steep rates
(or learn to hit that curveball), but you probably already know who
they are. Among the rest of your employees, if you have any doubts
about someone's ability to cope with your current growth and size,
you must confront the fact that they are not going to be able to help
lead you to your next level of scale.

Check your loyalty quotient. If you find yourself counting loyalty among an executive's top qualities, that should give you pause.
It's all too easy to fall into the trap of mistaking loyalty for competence as an organization scales.

Compounding the problem is that long-term executives tend to
play up their outstanding loyalty as a compensation for their struggles
in other areas. They will naturally try to embed themselves as irre-
placeable members of the team because the job they currently have is
way better than any they could get elsewhere. When retaining the job
at your company means more to an employee than that employee's
value to the company, you need to consider making a change.

And recalling the value of questions, one useful exercise in
evaluating your current team is to ask yourself whether a new boss

replacing you would hire your current executives, with their current resumes, into their current positions.

"Ask yourself whether a new boss replacing you would hire your current executives, with their current resumes, into their current positions."

Oftentimes early-stage executives would never be viable candidates for their own jobs if you were to go out in the market to fill this position today. Netflix has this evaluation process built into its talent management procedures, by asking managers to review their teams twice a year and determine if they have the optimal hire in each role. Netflix pays out a generous severance to anyone who is not ranked as an optimal hire, which may sound brutal, but it is the method by which Netflix has continually upgraded its team as the business has scaled.

The Netflix process acknowledges that as a company keeps scaling upward, the challenges ahead are going to require skills, talents, and levels of experience that weren't available to the company when it was smaller. Inevitably that means that a lot of the great people who enabled you to succeed so far are going to need to be replaced in order for you to grow. Even among those who are talented and capable of learning new skills, there may be a resistance among some of these long-term employees to embrace new practices and question the old ways of doing things—both of which will be key management competencies as you scale.

ROOM AT THE TOP

The other hazard you face by allowing employees with limited experience and capabilities to occupy important positions is that you leave little room for adding new talent. Founders tend to reward their loyal long-tenured employees with promotions and highfalutin titles. The truth is that it's highly unlikely that an early-stage employee will leave after being denied a more important title. On the other hand, by putting under-qualified people in lofty titled roles, you're sowing the seeds for problems later, possibly forcing their firing. These employees might have been better off if you had left room to hire a more experienced person into a higher-titled role, giving the long-term employees their chance to grow under new mentorship. If you are serious about growth, you must remember that it is better for everyone to resist raising an early-stage employee to an executive title than to try to remediate the situation later.

> *"If you are serious about growth, you must remember that it is better for everyone to resist raising an early-stage employee to an executive title than to try to remediate the situation later."*

Despite this, I've seen many founders attempt to solve this dilemma by inserting a new executive over the long-term employee, effectively demoting that employee while retaining an obsolete title. No matter how it appears on the surface, a demoted employee rarely becomes a satisfactory performer in a diminished role. The bruise to one's ego and status within the company is just too great. Most demoted team members will accept the initial decision, because there is no other similar position waiting for them outside your company. But then all too many of them end up aggrieved and disgruntled, poisoning your culture. They may even disparage and undermine the new executive who replaced them, believing that their loyalty will ultimately prevail.

My advice for employees who face demotions of this kind is that they negotiate as generous a severance as they can and leave. I call this "vote with your feet." Then I would offer the same advice I've given many executives that I've personally ushered out the door. Take stock of your true capabilities, assess your personal marketability, and find a new challenge outside this company—a place where you can start fresh.

Shedding long-term employees in this way is a healthy process, very much like the shedding of the snake's skin I referred to in the previous chapter. There is so much at stake that you can't afford to keep employees ill matched for your future challenges merely because they were invaluable in the past. If newly hired employees see that not-so-effective employees are retained and rewarded for their loyalty and tenure, your culture and team performance will suffer. Then, over time, your best people will leave in search of more meritocratic workplaces and you'll be left to run the company with your ineffective loyalists.

If guilt is a factor in retaining your long-term employees, consider assuaging it, just like Netflix, with generous severance packages. You know by now how reluctant I am to part with cash unnecessarily. But when it comes to easing out a loyal long-term employee, it is wholly appropriate to reward that loyalty with a parting gift of sorts, a bonus beyond their stock options, assuming they have stock options that are worth anything. If an employee is a drag on productivity and setting a poor example in the high-performance culture you're attempting to nurture, paying that person to leave is the most cost-effective course of action. At one firm where I was CEO, a board member persuaded me that the founder's brother needed to be ousted from his executive position for this very reason. Removing him ended up requiring a great deal of tact, diplomacy, and a more generous severance package than I had ever previously considered, but the organization desperately needed a talent upgrade in his critical role. Ultimately, allowing the founder's brother to leave quietly and well compensated was the right thing to do for him, for the founder, for me, and for the organization as a whole.

FIGHTERS, NOT LOVERS

As I've discussed, it's hard to assess your team's abilities in a clear light if you've all been together for a long time, so you need to get some help in discerning who will go and who should stay. If you find the process of objectively evaluating your senior staff's performance unsavory, then it's time to replace yourself with someone who sees the company's needs clearly enough to make the changes you can't bring yourself to.

> *"If you find the process of objectively evaluating your senior staff's performance unsavory, then it's time to replace yourself with someone who sees the company's needs clearly enough to make the changes you can't bring yourself to."*

Two decades ago, I was brought in as CEO at one company for just that purpose, though it wasn't clear to me at the start. I had been working closely with the founder for a number of months, when one afternoon our lead board member stopped by and invited me out to dinner. After small talk and cocktails, he asked bluntly if I would be willing to take on the CEO position, with the founder moving up into the chairman role.

No sooner had I agreed that I was up for the challenge than the board member quizzed me on what I intended to do about the sales department. Sales had been lagging for months, a source of concern throughout the company, and without much hesitation I told him I thought we needed to replace the sales vice president, who had worked closely with and been hired by the founder. The board member agreed and asked how long it would take me to accomplish that. I realized then that this was most likely the reason I was being so urgently offered a promotion. The company was in trouble, sales were stalled, the vice president of sales was probably long past his expiration date—but our founder could not bring himself to part ways with his loyal handpicked lieutenant. I believe it was less painful for the founder to hand off the CEO title than have to handle the dirty work himself—hence my promotion.

What the company needed, right at that moment, was someone who could not just identify the changes required, but had the finesse and the balls to make the changes. Someone who was willing and capable to stir things up and rebuild a newer, stronger, and more capable organization that would be prepared to take on new challenges. There were other good reasons why it was time for the founder to graduate to chairman, but in the very short term, the company needed a CEO to look at the organization with fresh eyes and make some moves that were long overdue. Decisiveness on personnel questions requires a tolerance for the hard feelings that arise from firings and resignations. If you thrive on positive feelings, then you may not be naturally suited for all the conflict and negative emotions inherent in scaling up your company.

For that reason, if you are a founder or a board member who is looking for a CEO successor, be sure to select someone who is not afraid to sever relationships of long-tenured employees who seem to be more valuable as a buddy than as an employee. I commonly divide executives into two personality types: lovers and fighters. Founders are almost always lovers; that is why, for my money, their best successor is likely a fighter.

"Losing him would be a monumental loss of institutional knowledge."

The board was about to announce a new CEO at a very challenging time. The company was on the verge of a large acquisition that had been overseen by the exiting founder, someone with two decades of tenure in the position. Some board members doubted the wisdom of letting go of all that institutional knowledge at such a critical moment. They considered keeping the founder on board as a paid consultant to shepherd the integration with the acquired company. They even debated postponing the new CEO's promotion for several months.

After some considerable agonizing, the board decided to make a clean break with the founder, without delay. The consensus was that the vast institutional knowledge of the departing executive might be more of a hindrance than a benefit. With the company almost doubling in size thanks to the new acquisition, the founder's skills and experience wouldn't have a place in such a large organization. Instead, they encouraged the newly appointed CEO to consider bringing in a new set of executives, skilled in integrating big mergers, people who could bring new ideas and fresh perspectives to the C-suite.

The past is interesting, but we know the future of a growing organization will be different. What matters most is what is needed *next* to scale your company—and by definition, that's nothing like what you've done in the past. Institutional knowledge can be very useful when navigating day-to-day decisions, but institutional knowledge tends to inhibit new thinking when it comes to setting strategies for growth and scale. Markets don't stand still. Technology keeps forging ahead. Competition keeps shifting and taking new forms. The role of the founder is to pursue relentless improvement in the face of change, and institutional knowledge is of dwindling value in such circumstances. Climb the ladder.

You need a culture that questions everything, all the time. A culture that is fraught with the curiosity to ask *why*, not cite precedent about what's worked in the past. Your team needs to serve as your propulsion, and that inevitably means you should have a regular cadence of turnover in the executive ranks as you grow. Without it, you run the risk of being like the shark that stops moving forward. You die!

I worked for a founder who suffered significant angst going through the period of transition, as the company scaled upward and required entirely new systems, new competencies, and new executives. I was brought in to handle that. Over the course of several years, virtually every member of this founder's executive team was transitioned out and replaced. They were not bad people, in fact, far from it—just the wrong skill sets for the challenges to come. We were in severe need of molting.

The very last one to go was a very loyal employee of almost twenty years' tenure. When I raised the prospect of this executive's termination, the founder demurred. "This goes beyond business," he implored. "He's my best friend in the company." The founder asked me to sleep on the decision, and the next morning when he returned, the founder agreed to the separation. He understood that the decision was very necessary to the success of the company. In the following year, the company's performance did indeed accelerate, but the founder had had enough. His angst over the changes caused him to throw in the towel and let someone else run the company.

There is no pussyfooting around the fact that as you bring on more people who are better suited for your company's next evolution, the people who helped build your company will seem more out of place.

"As you bring on more people who are better suited for your company's next evolution, the people who helped build your company will seem more out of place."

Except for the rare few who can grow their abilities with the company, you have to accept that the longer you keep people around who are not up to the task of building your company's future, the harder it will be for your best people to do what you hired them for.

TALENTED TERRORS

These hard lessons about tenure vs. ability are especially true in the case of your long-tenured "talented terrors" or, in the Netflix company term, "brilliant jerks." Every workplace has bad-behaving people who owe their job security to their seeming irreplaceability. These are the extremely valuable employees who hold some type of unique talent. Often they have technical backgrounds and single-handedly have authored some critical component of your product, but they abusively trample over lesser-skilled peers in their departments. Or they may be a salesperson who sells more than anyone else in your organization but who sucks more than her fair share of resources to support her efforts. Or anyone else who is valuable but just plain old offensive to work with.

Managers might warn you that if that valuable jerk of an employee were to leave it would wreak havoc and set your organization back years, but the toll they take on the company's culture is much worse.

"Managers might warn you that if that valuable jerk of an employee were to leave it would wreak havoc and set your organization back years, but the toll they take on the company's culture is much worse."

Their impact ranges far wider than their defined role, and the bulk of the damage they do is like that of an iceberg, unseen and below the waterline. Others in the organization avoid them. Some adopt the same "talented terror" habits because there seem to be no sanctions for bad behavior. At their worst, they sabotage the company by withholding information and resist training others in order to retain their reputation for irreplaceability.

Making the call on replacing a talented terror requires guts. All of the instincts and advice you will get will tell you not to make this move. Losing this talent will cost your organization dearly, but my advice is still to clear them out and take the hit. You indeed lose out on a specific skill or current capability, but another dozen or more people who have been victims of the talented terror will thank you for it with multiplied productivity and increased contributions to your culture, ultimately overcoming any capabilities that may have been lost.

CHANGE AT THE TOP

Turning over the organization in these ways will inevitably scare the rank and file, because almost everyone craves stability in the workplace. Most organizations are reticent to seize opportunities to change and improve because change is difficult. As a result, since 1955 the *Fortune* 500 has seen 88 percent of its ranks replaced, and the rate of replacement keeps growing from one decade to the next. Much of this turnover is due to established organizations getting bogged down in the quicksand of established institutional policies. Big firms commonly hang on to their institutional knowledge and put themselves at a disadvantage against newer, nimbler competition, and that's good news for startup founders with the emotional strength to not fall victim to the same dynamic.

I ran headlong into this fear within the rank and file when I took over the CEO role at Transcentive. When I addressed employees for the first time as CEO, we had just fifty or so employees, but our offices were so cramped that the only location that would physically accommodate that many people was the front reception area.

I knew this announcement would create some anxiety among our employees. Mike had founded and run the company for sixteen years. Change is hard, and despite the fact that I knew all the employees, I figured that replacing Mike was not going to be easy for them. So I very gently and cautiously laid out my ideas for what was going to change. I acknowledged the family atmosphere that we had enjoyed for sixteen years of Mike's leadership. Then I offered my approach, that of a performance culture, one that could provide increased opportunity as we grew and scaled the company together. Those who were willing to embrace change could look forward to expanding their experience and perhaps the contents of their wallets if we were able to accomplish what I envisioned.

Without so much as a pause after making that statement, Cora Keels, the long-tenured receptionist and long-term buddy of Mike's, piped up immediately and asked: "What if we liked it better before?" It was a good question, one shared by others who didn't speak up that day. Many in the room never quite got over the loss of the family atmosphere with me as CEO, and although Cora herself remained at Transcentive long after I had left, others in the room that day were gone within the year.

Change begins at the top, with a leader who is bold enough to declare a new direction, and everyone in the organization is free to choose whether they prefer the future or the past.

"Change begins at the top, with a leader who is bold enough to declare a new direction, and everyone in the organization is free to choose whether they prefer the future or the past."

By the way, I thanked Cora for her honest feedback. Although this was almost twenty years ago, Cora and I are still friends.

ONE IS THE LONELIEST NUMBER

"Asking for help will make me appear weak."

I often go back to my alma mater, Union College, to speak with undergraduate students. I recognize that my formative years in college contributed much to my life and career, so I feel an obligation to give back whenever I can. Some years ago, after giving a guest lecture there, I was approached by a student named Josh DeBartolo, who requested my advice on a startup idea he had. We discussed his idea at some length, and now, thinking back on it, his idea was uncannily similar to what Facebook turned out to be and was years before it became popular. Oh, well!

Although his business career path following graduation took Josh off the startup route, I was impressed with him enough that we stayed in touch. Over the years, Josh reached out to me periodically for advice and professional guidance. During a business trip to Salt Lake City, where Josh was working with Goldman Sachs at the time, we had the opportunity to get together in person to talk about his career. I proposed a meeting in Park City where we could combine our discussion with some snowboarding. Josh didn't know how to snowboard, and despite my three decades more of "maturity," or age disadvantage, he endeared himself further by asking me to teach him. I believe they call people like me "grays on trays." What impressed me about Josh was his coachability, his willingness to request help and advice, to take it in and then act on it.

We are often reticent to ask for help for fear of looking weak and surrendering our sense of control. We suspect people might think less of us if we reveal what we don't know. But in Josh's case and in countless other instances I've experienced, on either side of "the ask," that's rarely the impression that help-seekers give off. If you're like most people, you enjoy responding to a request for help and advice, and feel glad to have the opportunity. It's nice to be acknowledged for your skills and knowledge. The truth is that when you ask for help, it's likely that the person you ask will see you as someone who is humble, resourceful, eager to learn—and someone with excellent taste in choosing people to ask for help!

In 2016, almost a decade after I first met him, I offered Josh a job at Purview as one of our rising young executives. I've grown to know and respect him over the years out of conversations he initiated by requesting advice and guidance. I feel that Josh's future is only as limited as his ambitions, because I know him to be a capable, inquisitive leader who will always reach out for assistance when the situation warrants.

These qualities of Josh's are valuable for anyone to have, and for founders in particular, such qualities can be critical. Founders need to ask for help and advice because their job is inherently very isolating, with so many decisions left up to the founder alone. Most founders, however, prefer to keep their own counsel, to avoid the appearance of being weak or not in full control.

Founders who excel at asking for help know better. They know that a collaborative leadership style can put a charge into their organization. Who doesn't love it when the boss asks for your help and advice? The boss is telling you that you and your expertise are worth the boss's time. That's how asking for help is actually a sign of strength and self-confidence. It takes strength to admit you don't know everything and want to learn.

"It takes strength to admit you don't know everything and want to learn."

It shows empathy and respect for other opinions and experiences. "We're all imperfect and we all have needs," the legendary college basketball coach John Wooden used to say. "The weak usually do not ask for help, so they stay weak."

BEN FRANKLIN EFFECT

Beyond the empathy and the lessons we learn by asking for help from others, research shows that being asked for help predisposes that person to positive feelings about the person making the request. While this seems backwards, the phenomenon has been dubbed the Ben Franklin Effect. According to legend, Franklin once purposefully asked a rival Pennsylvania legislator to loan him a rare book. Upon returning the book, Franklin thanked the legislator profusely.

Apparently his premeditated act worked to melt the animosity, and the man became a lifelong friend of Franklin's. The Ben Franklin Effect is often associated with cognitive dissonance theory that states: "People change their attitudes or behavior to resolve tensions or dissonance between their thoughts, attitudes, and actions."

Asking for help creates dissonance, and along with it power—for you and everyone around you. In many cases, as it did for Ben Franklin and for Josh, it can deepen a relationship. Probably the most impactful thing you can do in the next five minutes is to call up someone you respect and maybe wish you knew better. Ask him or her for help with a problem or an issue that's on your mind. They will be flattered that you asked, and you will likely learn something you didn't expect, or perhaps see your situation in a new light. The experience will leave you both better for it. And unlike so many other things on your plate, this to-do item will cost you nothing.

"I often make better decisions when I keep my own counsel."

In my experience, there are two types of founders: those who are sure they know how to be a CEO, and those who are sure that they don't. You may find this odd, but if I had to choose one of these two to invest in, I would always choose the latter. Self-confidence is a valuable quality, but founders who accept their own uncertainty about the job are much more likely to ask questions, consider alternatives, and get help. Those are the exact behaviors necessary to scale as a leader.

Soliciting and accepting input from others can help you reason through your thought processes and test your assumptions to ensure that you are being as objective as possible in your decision-making. Ultimately, you retain the responsibility of making critical decisions on your own, which can often be a lonely task. Arriving at a decision, however, doesn't need to be lonely. In fact, it shouldn't be.

> "Arriving at a decision . . . doesn't need to be lonely. In fact, it shouldn't be."

Several times in my career when I have been stumped by a problem, I have requested help from former colleagues who had expertise in the problem area. In one of my CEO roles, our sales process was in desperate need of an overhaul, so much so that I didn't quite know where to begin. I called an old colleague, Chuck Nolan at Hyperion Solutions, where I knew the sales team was top-notch, and he and his team were happy to share the secrets of their success—a structured and repeatable sales process that they diligently trained and retrained their sales team to follow. I ended up adopting much of Hyperion's process and even hired their sales training consultant, Rick McAninch, to help me build a high-performance sales team of my own.

It takes some humility to make calls of that kind, and you always risk polite rejection, but never forget the rewards that are possible when it's time to make the next call for help. If you're willing to put your ego on hold and accept advice for what it's worth—advice, not instruction—you will find that it's never necessary to confront your problems alone.

Soon after taking over from a founder in my first CEO position, the loneliness of being at the top struck me very quickly. I reached out to several of my former bosses, each of whom had headed a large publicly traded software company and were very glad to serve as my informal sounding board. I recall how one assured me that the leap I had made—from vice president to CEO—was the largest gulf I would ever have to cross in my career. Those simple words of advice stuck with me and helped me accept and appreciate my new role in the one chair in the organization where the buck always stops.

ASKING PEOPLE YOU DON'T KNOW

The people you count on for advice need not be limited to those you already know. I'm continually amazed to find young and inexperienced founders getting enthusiastic advice from well-known CEOs with whom they had little or no prior relationship. They made the connection just by reaching out and asking. Most of the great CEOs I know are willing to help a less experienced founder who has a sincere interest in learning and improving. A request for help is a compliment to them, and such a request is likely to ingratiate you with whomever you approach—but only if your interest in improving is genuine.

To be good at making tough decisions, every founder needs a sounding board of some kind. Sound decisions are the result of hearing many views that often contradict and carefully considering the weight and sources of all the arguments. Before taking any important issue to the board for approval, a smart founder gets opinions from employees, peers, mentors, and other subject matter experts who are willing to speak their mind to help the founder discover the truth.

Peer Groups

In this regard, by far the most reliable source of help I've found over the past fifteen years is structured CEO peer groups.

"By far the most reliable source of help I've found over the past fifteen years is structured CEO peer groups."

In one of my first CEO gigs, I decided I needed help. I knew that CEO groups existed, so I began to do a bit of research. Serendipitously, I received a call from Mark Helow, the organizer of a group then known as Inc. Eagles. We shared ideas about learning, compared recent books we had read, and generally hit it off. Soon thereafter, he encouraged me to join his group. I did and ended up receiving the most important education of my career.

In a peer group you get an opportunity to test your strategies in advance of presenting them to your board or your executives. When they are specifically set up in such a way that excludes competitors from the same industry and other conflicts of interest, CEO peer groups can be the safest and most valuable venue to get an unbiased diversity of views on your challenges.

Among other great advice, your peer group will not hesitate to tell you when there's a booger hanging from your nose. It's one of the few places where a group of smart people will do you the tremendous favor of telling you the truth. If the emperor has no clothes, if your fondest plans are seriously naïve or misguided, your group will let you know, because they understand that the rarest and most precious commodity in a founder's life is the unvarnished truth.

"The rarest and most precious commodity in a founder's life is the unvarnished truth."

Throughout my various tenures as CEO, I regularly relied on a CEO peer group to help me hone my strategy and execution. The mere act of preparing a presentation that shares my inner thoughts with other CEOs makes me sharpen my thinking. Taking the hard knocks from your peers, as I recall experiencing several times, may be humbling, but it sure beats the repercussions of making that same flawed first-draft presentation to your board.

It takes a special kind of humility to bring your ideas to a group of this kind, especially if you really want to maximize the benefits of their feedback. It's the same with mentors or anyone else you seek help from. The value of the advice you receive is directly proportional to how vulnerable you're willing to be when you receive it.

"The value of the advice you receive is directly proportional to how vulnerable you're willing to be when you receive it."

If you're too eager to impress your mentor or peer group, you'll refrain from presenting your ideas in a way that exposes the unflattering details. It's tempting to seek advice about how to extricate yourself from a tight spot while omitting the details about how your oversights and dumb mistakes helped get you there. The advice you get will be faulty at best, and deeply misleading at worst, if you avoid the gory details for fear of your peers thinking less of you.

In one of my first peer group meetings, I shared with my new friends that one of my personal goals was to get my golf handicap below thirty. My peers quickly informed me that if my handicap was above thirty, I should stop keeping a handicap. It's that kind of honest feedback that both helped my golf game and improved my business acumen.

Mike Shane, an early member of that CEO group, was exceptional in his willingness to honestly expose his own inexperience. Having worked in only one job his entire career, as head of the company he founded, he craved feedback in a sincere effort to accelerate his learning. I recall one of our early CEO peer group meetings, in which Mike presented a novel idea to reverse his company's fall in revenue by engineering a reverse-merger into a public company shell. He thought this would enable him to raise money in the public market to rescue him from what he felt was a dire situation. While this might have been a good idea for a healthy company that desired to skip the expensive and time-consuming step of an IPO (initial public offering) in order to raise public capital, it was a fool's game for a struggling company. My guess is that this was an opportune proposal given to Mike by a not-so-honest business broker who would make a nice fee on the transaction. The group viewed this more like two drunks leaning up against each other. Once one shifted, they both would crumble to the ground. It wasn't the stupidest idea I had ever heard, but it was right up there. His peers took his carefully prepared plan and shredded it.

To Mike's credit, that harsh feedback from the group compelled him to take stock and decide to confront the company's other problems. Forced to abandon his financial engineering shortcut, Mike rolled up his sleeves and took a hard look at his team. With the group's help and advice, Mike began to push his executives to raise their game, demand clearer performance metrics from the entire organization, and adopt systematic topgrading for evaluating new hires. The company's revenue picture turned around, allowing

Mike to make a strategic acquisition that significantly enhanced the company's market position. Not so many years later, Mike led his company through a successful sale to a global conglomerate. It was an extraordinary achievement that would not have been possible if, years earlier, Mike hadn't had the courage to air his "dumb idea," take in the criticism, and change his thinking.

"The board will think I'm in over my head if I let on how much I don't know."

A young executive I had been mentoring took on the CEO role from the founder of his organization. In the very first meeting with his board as CEO, he asked the board for their advice on his proposed strategy—in line with my advice, or so he thought. The board gave him exactly what he asked for. He was subjected to seven different opinions, many contradictory, from six different board members. After the meeting he came to me to nurse his wounds.

"I don't get it," he moaned. "I engaged the board to help me with feedback on my strategy and instead I am now more confused." It's true that I had advised him to actively solicit feedback from his board, but he'd asked in a way that was too vague and non-specific. I counseled him that he should have asked for their thoughts on the underlying assumptions of his strategy, rather than offer an opinion of what he'd done. Good boards probe the CEO's thought processes, rather than trying to rethink the CEO's conclusions, and that's the direction you want to steer your board members. You want to offer your board the opportunity to provide you with guidance to impact your thought process—not invite them to debate whether or not they agree with your strategy.

"You want to offer your board the opportunity to provide you with guidance to impact your thought process—not invite them to debate whether or not they agree with your strategy."

Asking the board, "Did I assess my performance correctly?" is a better question than "What do you think?" Board members want to know about the assumptions you made in forming your strategy. More importantly, they want to be sure you haven't overlooked something important. They want to know that you know! That's why I've always found that my preparation for a board meeting is at least as important as the meeting itself.

In pure corporate governance parlance, your board is your boss, and as a boss yourself, you know that you don't want clueless employees asking you to tell them what to do. You want your employees to take responsibility for results, which is exactly what your board wants from you. My friend from Goldman Sachs would agree that the statement "There are no dumb questions" is decidedly not true when it comes to your board, as my young mentee learned.

Founders who get the most from their board meetings are those who know going in that the board wants your objective evaluation of your own performance. They don't care much about external factors beyond your control—increased-duration customer buying cycles, rising interest rates, or the direction of the economy. If you want to maintain your board's confidence, don't risk wasting their time making excuses, even in the most extreme cases.

One of the most personal memorable board meetings I've ever experienced took place on October 3, 2001, just three weeks after the 9/11 terror attacks on the World Trade Center and the Pentagon.

I had missed a solid week in the office because I had been stuck overseas with no flights to return home. Our results that quarter were already down significantly due to the hangover effects of the dotcom bust. The world was reeling, and uncertainty in the markets had prompted a near-total freeze in corporate capital investments—bad news for business software companies like ours.

And yet, on the day of this meeting, my board members only wanted to hear one thing from me: How were we going to get our performance back on track?

I wasn't prepared at all for this question because, I admit, I entered that meeting expecting to get a free pass for that quarter. But none of these extenuating circumstances were of any interest to my board members. I found it maddening to have to respond to their questions that day, during such a chaotic time. But it drove home a message that I've never forgotten. Your job as CEO is to create positive results and to take complete responsibility if you fall short of that expectation.

> "Your job as CEO is to create positive results and to take complete responsibility if you fall short of that expectation."

The buck does stop with the CEO.

Boards expect you to make decisions, provide your rationale and consideration, and execute. They expect you to ask them for help in areas of their expertise, prepare them for their meetings, and take their feedback to heart. No self-respecting board member wants to make your decisions for you. A board member colleague of mine once described the typical board member's approach as this: "Just show up and whine." Hopefully your board is better than that, but the principles are the same. The founder presents, and the board members critique and complain . . . or, should I say, "give the gift of feedback"?

ALIGNING WITH YOUR BOARD

The picture is complicated by the fact that even diligent, responsive board members have other interests not aligned with yours or the company's, despite their legal fiduciary responsibility to represent the interests of *all* of the shareholders. It's great to have a board member who's also a customer, for instance, as a source of insight about your market, but it's also likely that that board member's advice will reek of self-interest. Major investors on the board, including venture capitalists and angel investors, are always more concerned about the specific returns to themselves and their partners. Family board members may be focused on the employment status of their executive kin. I had a board member from a venture capital firm nearly blow up a somewhat fragile deal to sell the company because at the last minute he decided that his partners deserved an extra $1 million beyond his originally agreed-upon consideration and in excess of the price the other shareholders had agreed upon.

Fear of these and other complications are among the reasons so many founders delay or utterly avoid the creation of a substantial board of directors. They tend to see a board as a source of unwanted intrusion on their personal decisions. Perhaps worse are the founders who go ahead and create a board, but then fill it with family members, friends, and cofounders to ensure a virtual rubber stamp on their actions. This is just a waste of the founder's and board's time.

Such founders can't possibly know what they've been missing.

Once you see past the prejudices and parochial interests, good boards can also help you get to the truth. They maintain effective bullshit alerts for the times when your natural inclination is to short-circuit your decision process without doing the homework necessary to consider the alternatives. When founders and their boards get aligned on scaling their organizations, they can develop a relationship that is highly functional and collaborative.

"When founders and their boards get aligned on scaling their organizations, they can develop a relationship that is highly functional and collaborative."

And board members are always there to help, if you make effective requests for help. Early in my tenure at Transcentive, it was clear that our sales performance was lagging, and my approach with the board was to ask them to help me come up with an alternative. Instead of presenting my strategy and asking for their approval, I asked for introductions to companies from which we might be able to learn. By soliciting their help in my education, they gladly took up the role of mentors and put aside their roles as judges and evaluators.

Most importantly, by drawing from the information I gathered from the board's contacts, I was able to propose a sales reorganization strategy that the board members had already participated in. By enrolling their help early in the process, I offered the board "ownership" of what I had proposed. Later, when the strategy worked and our sales took off, the board and I also shared the victory, having worked together as a team in overcoming one of the company's most serious problems.

"If I have to solicit all those opinions, it will slow us down."

I serve on the board of a company with a founder that has a great habit of meeting selectively with certain board members in advance of an upcoming board meeting. I think he picks the board members that might give him the most trouble in our meetings; perhaps that's why he calls me. In these one-on-one sessions, he goes over proposals and concepts he expects will arouse objections from these particular board members. He uses this opportunity to test-run his ideas, tease out objections, and prepare himself with winning arguments in advance of making a formal proposal for action. Just as importantly, he requests help. Having learned the lessons from Ben Franklin, by enrolling these board members in the preparation phase of his thought processes, he is able to gain their support for proposals they would likely have taken issue with (and possibly shot down) if their first look had been at an open meeting.

The one thing all boards hate is surprises—even good surprises.

"The one thing all boards hate is surprises—even good surprises."

A smart founder who is aware of this tendency among board members can seize the opportunity to engage with the board proactively. Rather than crafting board books with spun tales of greatness, founders who point out their disappointing results and honestly assess their progress are more apt to find an empathetic audience. Telling it like it is and seeking counsel on your strategic response builds credibility. If you engage your board with a mutual goal of incremental improvement, that is a much better use of your board's collective knowledge than asking the board to rubber-stamp your existing strategy.

Unfortunately, all too many early-stage companies who do assemble boards populate them with "friendlies." Too many are composed of cofounders, family, and friends who are grateful to serve and do little to hold the founder accountable. As I continue to rediscover, these boards are less valuable than not having a board at all.

Monthly or quarterly board meetings, after all, are not supposed to be love fests, even if that's what every founder would prefer. If all you're doing is seeking peace through consensus and compromise, you risk missing opportunities to split with the status quo, when that's what the circumstances call for. The most successful founders are those who are willing to question the board's outlook, but they do it by engaging in informal advance discussions. Having pointed out that the board is technically the boss, bosses too need to be managed—not manipulated. Collectively, boards put up resistance at the first sign that a founder is trying to coerce them into taking action contrary to their expectations. But most board members are open to challenging discussions individually, well before they are expected to take a formal vote.

If the above seems like a fairly commonsense approach to board management, you'd be amazed how uncommonly it is practiced. Founders, in particular, are much more likely than most CEOs to spring ideas as surprises at board meetings. Boards tend to tolerate this behavior from founders because investors on those boards need to be seen as founder-friendly if they want to keep making investments in startups. As a result, you may have your growth stunted by overly indulgent boards. Many startups fail simply because board members give you far too much rope—until the rope is finally long enough to strangle you and the entire enterprise.

Rob, an engineer I know well, was promoted to CEO of an advanced materials manufacturer after the board had grown so frustrated with the founder that he was finally removed. The company had been flailing, having entered and exited bankruptcy in recent years. Ownership was now consolidated into a couple of private equity investors who were losing interest in what was now a tired investment. The future of the company was not certain.

Rob is an engineer's engineer—extraordinarily thoughtful and solution oriented. He was well steeped in the disciplines of product development and the technical details of the manufacturing process, but he knew what he didn't know, too. He knew he had little or no expertise in the skills required for the CEO job. So Rob sought out a mentor to be a sounding board for the most prickly decisions he was facing. I connected him with a CEO peer group, and over the next six years that group was invaluable in advising him and helping him think through his priorities. For instance, his peer group convinced him to shake up his sales staff when, as a new CEO with no experience in sales, he was reluctant to give up on the team he'd inherited. He ended up replacing key executives in other departments, too.

Rob's mentor and the peer group also helped him formulate a strategy for recapitalizing the company, which was a very tricky issue to take to a board of directors filled with entrenched investors. He developed a bold plan to buy out non-committed shareholders at above-market value, issuing company debt to purchase their shares. Non-committed investors that stayed would remain minority owners with little say over the direction of the company.

Within three years, his company was growing by double digits, and sales and profits had both increased five-fold since the day the new CEO took over. When I last checked in with Rob, he and his board were considering a liquidity event that (thanks to the company's improved capital structure) stands to make the CEO and his loyal investors extremely rich. It's the best story I know of how a smart but inexperienced CEO has been able to succeed magnificently because he excels at asking for advice and taking in a lot of opinions and perspectives before moving ahead.

The sad thing is that the founder of the company could have achieved the same things if only he'd been more resourceful and coachable when it came to seeking help and advice. He had built this business from scratch, invented many of the processes the company still uses today, and initiated many of the company's key customer relationships. But none of that was enough to make him a successful CEO. It was the willingness of his replacement to acknowledge his lack of managerial expertise, to seek help and engage with his board, that emboldened him to shake up the executive ranks and realign the ownership structure. By doing so, Rob ultimately took the company where its founder never could.

SEVEN

WITHOUT YOU

"The company requires my personal attention in order to scale."

When Paul Thompson joined our CEO peer group in early 2005, there was something about him that made him stand out from the rest of us. As the founder of the North Carolina tech company Transportation Insight, he seemed much less involved in the day-to-day business of his company than most of us thought was possible or even desirable. He appeared detached, almost aloof, from TI's operations. Some of us suspected he didn't really have much on the ball.

For instance, Paul had uniformly high regard for all the executives on his team, expressing almost no serious concerns about any of them. One of the most important exercises during our quarterly meetings was to grade our key executives with A, B, or C ratings and then discuss our evaluations with the group. Through this process, most of us discovered we'd rated our own executives a little too high. We all tended to give them passes for performance issues that really needed to be addressed. The value of the exercise was that our peers would help us take off the rose-colored glasses and identify areas requiring improvement. Paul, however, not only gave his executives exceptionally high grades, he also was very persuasive in defending his assessments.

What none of us realized at the time was that Paul was probably the best prepared among all of us in scaling his company, climbing The Founder Value Ladder, and launching it on its way to its next level. Paul's A-team of executives at Transportation Insight ran the company without his daily meddling because that was his plan. He put those A-level players in the right seats and then he got out of the way, which allowed him to focus purely on the strategic direction of the company. He reduced TI's dependency on himself as its founder, and in doing so clearly separated his personal identity from that of the company.

Paul did way more than delegate his authority to his very capable team. Instead, he did what the blog *From Founder to CEO* in its "50 Shades of Delegation" article calls "enlisting others to be the delegates of the mission." This has a much higher and more impactful result than simple task delegation. It's more about enrolling a team in owning the mission of the company. None of us in Paul's CEO peer group could appreciate this at the time. An approach like his runs contrary to the way most founders see themselves in relation to their companies. At the stage of development that TI was in at the time, most founders are deeply involved in the day-to-day, intimately involved in almost every aspect of operations and carrying the corporate flag. Paul instead got his team to lead the charge.

It's the kind of intimate involvement in a growing, successful firm that also tends to feed the founder's ego. An emotional bond can form between the founder and the company that may complicate plans for future separation. Sometimes founders commingle their personal finances with that of the company because they see no difference between the two. Employees, customers, and vendors come to view the company as the founder's personal domain—and interact with the company on that basis.

Then, when a company's growth trajectory calls for transformational change, all these factors make it much more difficult for the founder to follow through. Making the changes necessary to scale the organization can be so disruptive and upsetting at this point— to the organization and to themselves—that many founders put it off indefinitely, and some never make the changes at all. In the process, they betray their own dreams for themselves and their families.

Paul, by contrast, never had to change his style in order to get his company to scale. At the earliest stage possible, he brought in great people to take on key responsibilities. Then he focused his attention on the next rung up on The Founder Value Ladder. He spent his time focused on strategy around the company's future opportunities. The role of the company in his life was not to feed his ego, but to generate wealth for himself and his stakeholders.

> *"The role of the company in his life was not to feed his ego, but to generate wealth for himself and his stakeholders."*

He always acted on the belief that the organization was bigger than any one individual. Paul intended to build a strong company that would live on without him, and then he took action to ensure that he had a good life waiting for him after that transition.

"I don't have time for anything else other than this business."

What Paul Thompson did was build a long runway so his company could gradually gain lift and leave the ground, away from himself and his personal identity. Today his role with Transportation Insight mostly involves exploring acquisitions that would make the company stronger. He's executing on the final, orderly phase of his exit from the company at the highest rung of The Founder Value Ladder as an investor, looking for ways to leverage his corporate assets to grow the company. From the top of the ladder, he's got the optimal perspective of his company. As he recently told me, he is working toward no longer being needed because he will have ensured the company's future success.

If you are serious about scaling your company, it's never too early to start thinking in terms that align with transitioning you out of it. The longer the runway, the better. You can't really go wrong if you undertake each executive search with the goal of finding someone capable of replacing you someday. It's the most valuable form of business insurance imaginable.

Long runways provide your eventual successor with exposure to all the actual responsibilities associated with the CEO role. If you take this first step early enough, you will have the opportunity to hold a long audition. Maybe you'll discover after a period of time that your planned successor is not an ideal fit after all and that you can do better. Hiring your planned successor early gives you a chance at a mulligan (for you non-golfers, that is a penalty-free do-over) if that individual is exposed as a poor fit. You have time to go out and try again to find the right person because you started looking early.

"Hiring your planned successor early gives you a chance at a mulligan if that individual is exposed as a poor fit."

At Purview, barely two years into my tenure as CEO, I've already added Josh, whom I described earlier as someone who has the potential to be my successor. I had several objectives in selecting him. I wanted an executive from a completely different background than mine, someone who could ask those naïve questions an industry pro wouldn't be comfortable asking. I also wanted someone who would take the time to learn this industry, and make some mistakes along the way with a safety net below. And finally, I also wanted to be sure that this was the right personality for the job. With a long runway, I can see whether others in the organization would be comfortable with his executive leadership if that time should come.

TRY BEFORE YOU BUY

There is no better way to test a potential successor than to spend years working with that person in the course of a planned succession. It's a simple concept I call *try before you buy*.

Hiring, after all, is a highly error-prone process. We've all hired "can't miss" executives who turn out to be duds. In fact, I've hired many more duds than I care to admit. One of my board members, Bob Sywolski, says that you're ahead of the game if your hiring success rate is 50 percent. That sounds dismal, but I console myself that no one in major league baseball ever hits .500, and that even three successes out of ten tries can land a hitter in the Hall of Fame. Hopefully, my hiring record is better than that.

You will recall in Chapter Three that we discussed founders who got off The Founder Value Ladder at the lowest rungs and gave way to other executives who led their companies to fame and fortune. What might have missed your attention is that two of these cases, Cisco and LinkedIn, both failed in their first attempt to hire the right successor for their founder(s). Cisco hired John Morgridge, who had previously run GRiD. But in 1995 Morgridge gave way to John Chambers, who then very successfully led Cisco for two decades until 2016. Similarly, Reid Hoffman originally hired Dan Nye as his successor, who lasted but two years as CEO and was succeeded by the much better-known and also very successful Jeff Weiner.

Hiring mistakes are expensive. In some ways, you almost can't put a price on the opportunity costs you suffer when the wrong person takes up space for a time at the head of a unit or a department. Some HR professionals peg the cost of a bad hire as high as fifteen times an executive's salary when those opportunity costs are taken into account.

So testing these relationships in advance, including all the conflicts and differences of opinion that no doubt will arise, is a critically important consideration for any succession. Not having this runway leaves you guessing how the relationship will evolve. Winning the confidence to be a successor to a founder is a difficult task for both the founder and the successor.

Ensuring that the successor will protect the legacy of the founder while still pursuing the bold new initiatives necessary to scale the organization is a tall order for any succession. Twice, I've had the opportunity to start as an executive in a company where I later succeeded the founder. Both times, before I was promoted to CEO it was clear that the founder and I had developed a sufficiently trusting relationship to enable me to do the job. In each case it was also clear that the founder was comfortable with my very different style. The runway we had built gave them that opportunity.

For that reason, runways can be very long. In 2006, The Metro Group in Long Island City, New York, hired a young up-and-coming executive, Richard Parker, whom the board identified as a potential successor to the then-CEO. Over the years since his hiring, Parker had been given a growing set of responsibilities and educational opportunities, each of which he took on with passion and professional zeal. He was finally named to the CEO position at the end of 2015. And by initial measurements, he was both the right person for the job and someone who could take the company to its next level. This long runway gave the shareholders of this family-owned, closely held company the chance to develop the deep level of trust required of the first non-family CEO in more than eighty years.

CHARISMATIC FOUNDERS NEED EVEN LONGER RUNWAYS

In general, the more dynamic and charismatic a founder is, the more difficult it will be to find the right candidate to succeed her. As a result, succession plans for these types of founders are usually non-existent, even though there's a case to be made that this type of founder is more in need of a long runway than any other kind.

Not-for-profit organizations can have these succession problems as well. One of the companies I worked with was involved with a very worthy charity in the Baltimore–Washington, DC, area, the Children's Cancer Foundation (CCF). The foundation had been launched thirty years earlier by Shirley Howard, a driven, diminutive woman who, through the sheer force of her personality, had accumulated over $30 million in donations with little staff and minimal overhead.

Shirley was a fireball. In every way, other than her physical size, she was larger than life. An executive from one of the major donor organizations told me Shirley was so persistent that they would commit their funds to CCF just to make her go away. Anyone who knew CCF knew Shirley. She attended every fund-raising event personally. She touched every donor and virtually every donee. Video of Shirley was on the front page of the website. Shirley was the Children's Cancer Foundation.

In 2014, Shirley passed away. All at once, operations at the CCF came to a screeching halt. In Shirley's absence, no one knew what to do. No processes were documented. No database of donors existed. As CCF's board scurried to hire a professional executive director, Shirley's daughter played an interim role. Donations, in the meantime, plummeted.

It didn't have to be this way. The board of CCF should have insisted that Shirley have a succession plan in place. Every board needs to know who is ready to take over if the unthinkable should happen tomorrow, an idea so fundamentally important that it's come up several times before in this book.

"Every board needs to know who is ready to take over if the unthinkable should happen tomorrow."

Shirley's board did not prepare the organization for life after Shirley, and as a result all that Shirley had built was put at risk, endangering both her life's work and her legacy.

"I check in a few times every day when I'm away."

The best way to test your company's preparedness for succession is to take yourself out of the loop temporarily. Go on a vacation somewhere with poor or non-existent cell-phone service. If some of your operations prove themselves shaky while you're away, you'll get a good picture of where improvement is needed. More likely, though, you'll discover that much of your company works better without you.

After many years of trying to wean myself away from being in constant contact with the office, here are five important lessons I've learned:

1. **Matters that seem urgent rarely are.** Waiting to respond can often be just the tonic required for an urgent matter to resolve itself. Having this happen without having to call a fire drill, reprioritize, or engage in other unnatural acts is a much simpler way to solve problems.

2. **Your people will do the right thing without you.** And they'll usually do it more competently than you expect. Disconnecting gives the best of your people the opportunity to shine. They'll show what they can do, experience full responsibility, and learn to trust that you really trust them.

3. **You'll see your true effectiveness as a leader.** If you have articulated a clear Commander's Intent, like the generals at

Gettysburg, your people will very likely solve unexpected problems in ways you'd approve in your absence. And if they don't, you might want to take a second look at how effectively you've communicated your priorities.

4. **It's easier to see the big picture when you're away.** Distance clears your mind for thoughts about direction and strategy, thoughts that rarely have room to blossom in days filled with decisions and meetings. Richard Branson founded Virgin Airways upon returning from a Caribbean vacation, because delayed flights and poor service gave Branson ideas about how he'd do better. A world of inspiration awaits you away from the office.

5. **A stress test is healthy for the organization**. It will expose both strengths and weaknesses. An unplugged vacation can be yet another tool for getting to the truth of what's happening within the company.

In the past, whenever I took even a day away from the office, I remained tethered by cell phone and laptop. These were my twin umbilical cords, enabling me to stay in touch with what was going on. I always assumed this was the right and responsible thing to do. Nothing got lost or delayed, and I assumed the company was better for it. You probably do the same.

One of my good friends and colleagues, Kurt Johnson, founder of Horizon Technology, told me that after he started his company, he didn't take any time off for many years. Finally, having been harassed by his family to take a vacation, he took the whole company along on vacation with them. "I just didn't trust they could manage without me," he said. "So I made sure they were with me."

Some years later Kurt went on a cruise with just his family.

He recalls how he had counted on an online satellite connection aboard the ship to serve as his link back to the real world. But the connection was so slow it drove him crazy. On some days he could not connect at all with the office he left behind. He became angry and frustrated during what should have been a relaxing time with his family. Then, when he returned, he discovered that his company had hardly missed him. His people were better prepared and more self-reliant than he had ever realized.

I once had a similar experience. On family vacations, I used to get up early before my family and sneak down to the hotel lobby to check email from the prior day. On one such occasion, my cell phone stopped working. The office tried to contact me, per my instructions, but couldn't get through. I was fuming about the problem the entire day. Then, when I returned to the office, I was told while I was incommunicado, there had indeed been an urgent decision that needed my input. When they failed to reach me, however, someone else had to make the call. And that person handled it just fine.

That one instance of a cell-phone failure was the first of many lessons that took years to sink in. Looking back, I can see that almost all of my anxiety was self-inflicted. My constant checking in with the office annoyed my family, who wanted me to relax with them and enjoy our time together. I know this because they reacted to my work-related interruptions with scowls and snippy comments. What wasn't as clear to me at the time was that this checking-in and checking-up behavior was distracting and offensive to the people at the office, too. I had always told them how much I trusted them, but my behavior told them that I really trusted no one but myself.

"I had always told them how much I trusted them, but my behavior told them that I really trusted no one but myself."

When you leave town and trust your team to take care of the shop, you build their confidence. On the other hand, as long as you suspect the organization requires your presence for every important decision, your suspicions will no doubt be proved correct. To your employees, relying on you to make all the tough decisions is the path of least resistance. That passive mentality will prevail as long as you remain overly obsessed with control, so don't be surprised that some of your employees may lack drive and ambition. You've made it clear that only your drive and ambition matters.

There are two important danger signs that you are not building your runway to transition:

How many hours you work each week. Founders who continue to work insane hours (sixty or more) are likely controlling too many of the organization's decisions.

Excessive turnover in the organization. When capable employees have their authority and professional growth stifled by a controlling founder, they tend to leave.

Perhaps you don't think your team has earned their decision-making chops. Unfortunately, this too is a self-fulfilling prophecy—until you let them try, they will never show you proof. Grooming team members to get comfortable with accepting the responsibility of delegation requires you give them that opportunity. Learning to wean yourself from this addiction to control requires that you recognize the problem and exert the discipline needed to step back in an orderly, rational way.

Start Small: Disconnect Briefly

Put your cell phone down and go out for a walk. Try leaving it in your drawer at the office. Try not taking it into a meeting. If you really get bold, try leaving it at home for a day. Unhooking the umbilical cord is difficult for founders. I've been on the golf course with founders who checked in with the office between each hole—a few even checked their email between each swing. But the first step toward unhooking is to remove the temptation to check in. For that reason, I strongly recommend that you never, ever acquire an Apple watch, Pebble, or whatever is the latest Dick Tracy device. Having a conversation with a founder constantly interrupted as he consults the email streaming on his wrist only had to happen once for me to be convinced.

Delegate Some Authority

Next, try granting complete authority to someone in your organization to make any decisions that don't seem to belong to anyone else. I raised this issue in Chapter Three. In most companies, founders can drown in minutiae that ends up on their desk because it doesn't seem to belong to any other department. Make sure all these issues are assigned to someone you trust—ideally, a potential successor.

Plan a Meeting Without You

Next, initiate a company meeting but don't attend. Empower someone else in the company to craft the agenda and run the meeting. You can watch it remotely, if you want, as long as you don't participate. Witness your company operating without you.

Take a Vacation

Now, it's time for your vacation to that place with no cell-phone service. You can find a list of some great places to unplug at www.travelandleisure.com/blogs/best-vacation-spots-to-unplug. Assuming you have been able to keep yourself off the grid and let things happen as they will while you were gone, you may just return to find that there have been things that the organization has been capable of that you have been inhibiting. You may just find the organization is plenty ready to go on without you.

"This company can't run without me."

In 2012, Paul Thompson handed over Transportation Insight's CEO role to one of his A-team executives. Around that time, Paul and his partners recapitalized the company in partnership with a private equity firm based in nearby Charlotte, NC.

The recapitalization has helped Transportation Insight grow through acquisitions, but just as important, it enabled Paul and his stakeholders to take some shekels off the table without entirely giving up their stake in the future of the company. The infusion of cash from this handpicked investment firm made Paul and several of his executives wealthy, while allowing them to maintain the culture and direction that they worked so hard to build.

Paul was always ahead of the curve in empowering his team and moving toward his inevitable transition to the top rung of The Founder Value Ladder. Now, by removing much of his risk concentration in the shares he holds in the company, he's made it even easier to allow others to run the company, without his entire financial future staked on his company's performance.

RELIEVING THE PRESSURE

As hard as it is for any founder to let go of control over the company, it is especially hard when a founder has the vast majority of his or her net worth invested in the organization's success. The concentration of risk that most founders have in the value of their company stock exerts an enormous degree of pressure on them. With so much riding on the success of their company, founders are naturally reluctant to give up control and authority.

Of course, on the other hand, investors prefer their founders to also be deeply invested in the success of the organization. Buyers and investors often worry that allowing the founder to take too much money out of the deal will sap the founder's drive. But savvy board members and successor CEOs have come to realize that this level of pressure can have a negative effect on the founder's willingness to delegate decision-making. Enabling the founder to take some of his equity off the table is a way to lessen this angst and lubricate delegation decisions. A partial equity buyout is a way to relieve some of this pressure.

More than once I've heard a founder remark after taking some investment out of a company: "At least I got something out of this, even if the company craters." But if you have enough money to allow you to sleep at night, the company is more likely to run in a sane and orderly way. That's because, as I've learned, for the founder, the psychological impact of taking money off the table is far greater than the practical financial advantage of diversifying one's holdings.

When I took over the reins at Transcentive, Mike Brody, the company's founder some sixteen years earlier, had a pretty tight grip on the company. Not much got past Mike, and not much got done without his scrutiny. A venture capital firm had just invested several million dollars in the company, and had even paid a portion of the proceeds directly to Mike. That wasn't common practice for VCs at the time, but Transcentive was already profitable and Mike such a mature manager that they made an exception.

The money was enough to convince Mike to allow the VC firm to join his board and begin to influence some of the direction of the company. But like most founders, Mike still had the vast percentage of his wealth tied up in the potential value of the company. And it made Mike anxious enough that his obsessive attention to details continued unabated.

Then, during the height of the dot-com boom, Mike and his founding team took advantage of an opportunity to sell some of their shares to several institutional customers. After that day, Mike was transformed. His desire to control and his anxiety vanished almost instantly. Mike's stake in the company was still large, but the infusion of cash from this stock sale took a ton of pressure off him. He took time off for the first time in years. He bought a house in Virginia and spent weeks at a time there, away from the office.

The palpable reduction in Mike's anxiety levels, brought on by the stock sale, inevitably made it easier for our whole management team to function, and the company thrived. We ended up selling the company five years later, finally allowing Mike to cash out his equity in the company, that big payday for years of hard work. Subsequently, Mike came back to run a product unit for us. Without the pressure of his net worth being tied to the company, Mike was free to enjoy contributing to strengthening that product line without any worries about the company's overall direction. Transcentive had been Mike's baby, and now the baby was all grown up and out of his house. He had developed a mature and healthy relationship with Transcentive, the kind any parent would want with their adult offspring.

ADJUST EARLY

The earlier you are able to recognize the inevitability that you will not be the head of your organization forever, the better. It takes a purposeful shift in organizational momentum to make the transition from a founder-led organization successfully, and without anticipating the financial and psychological impacts on the founder, it's impossible to prepare properly. The well-prepared founder senses when the music is about to stop and has a well-formulated plan for what's next for her and her organization. She has someone in place who is ready to assume her role.

Recently, I visited Paul Thompson in Hickory, North Carolina, to see how he and Transportation Insight were doing. Paul had just returned from a month-long trip to Mount Kilimanjaro with his daughter, and we met at the company's headquarters, a beautifully restored hosiery factory campus in the center of Hickory.

Paul now devotes all his time at Transportation Insight to making strategic acquisitions to fuel the company's growth. He holds four executive officer/board-level positions at three other companies, and serves on the board of non-profits that include Water to Wine, Samaritan's Feet, Hickory Christian Academy, and the Walker College of Business at Appalachian State University.

On the Transportation Insight website, Paul is identified as founder and chairman, but his picture is no more prominent than that of about twenty-five other faces on that page. So many founder-based companies I've encountered exalt the founder's achievements on their websites, but on the pages of Transportation Insight you'll have a hard time finding any indication that the company is in any way "Paul's company."

On the other hand, if you click on the image of his smiling face, Paul's brief biography begins by stating simply that "Paul Thompson is the vision behind Transportation Insight."

The accuracy of that statement is impeccable. Paul is not his company. He's not even its leader. He is the vision behind the leadership. He provides the vision that guides and supports the leadership's work. Like the wind beneath a bird's wings, Paul helps his company gain altitude, and succeeds in the task by doing so invisibly. That's the admirable endpoint that every transitioning founder should aim for.

EIGHT

PASSING THE TORCH

"Don't worry, I'll stay out of the way."

Not long after moving to the Annapolis area in Maryland, I inevitably acquired a boat. It's been said that a boat owner's second happiest day is the day he buys a boat—the happiest day being the day he later sells it. I guess I haven't yet had my happiest day. So far I have found owning a boat to be quite enjoyable, but maintaining it and keeping it clean is a lot of work.

Seagulls are the most persistent source of filth on my boat. Despite my best efforts to scare them off with rubber snakes and plastic owls, or to prevent them from perching by capping the pier pilings with pointed cones, the seagulls keep coming back to create a mess. The seagulls nest more permanently elsewhere, but the pier is their favorite place to hang out, leaving white gooey gifts all over the place before they fly off, blissfully unaware.

Founders who have been replaced as CEOs remind me of

seagulls. The company they founded is no longer their nest, but that doesn't stop most founders from coming by for a visit, making some mischief, and then gliding back out the door. I've affectionately named this behavior "seagulling." If they leave untidiness behind them, they're unaware because they're not around to take note. The mess they create is their successor's problem.

CAN YOUR PRIDE WEATHER A NEW ROLE?

When given a choice, a large majority of founders will do almost anything to stay involved with the ventures they founded, even if it means volunteering for a demotion. A Harvard Business School study of technology companies showed that upon the appointment of a new CEO, 70 percent of founders end up taking a lesser role at the ventures they founded, rather than departing. Some become chief technology officers. Others take on a role as special advisor to the CEO, a glorified consulting appointment. If they haven't been forced out entirely, most founders opt to stay involved.

If this describes you, then you need to ask yourself: Why? If you still have a large investment in the company, it's a reasonable desire to stay involved in hopes that you can still contribute. You naturally want to protect what could be a large liquidity opportunity in your future. But what may not be clear to you is how your being there in a diminished role will protect that investment.

No matter how you dress it up, any role you assume after your tenure as CEO is clearly a demotion.

"No matter how you dress it up, any role you assume after your tenure as CEO is clearly a demotion."

As a manager, if you've ever demoted anyone, you know that demotions rarely end well. It's human nature for a demoted employee to look critically at the person now doing his job. From the demoted employee's perspective, doing things differently is doing things wrong, even if it generates better results. Demoted employees are often not shy about sharing that assessment with their colleagues, fanning the embers of discord within your organization. I've found that a better approach would be to ante up some severance and terminate that employee quickly.

So it's a very rare demoted employee who can look at his or her replacement and say, "Wow, I would never have tried to do it that way. Brilliant!"

But that's exactly the attitude you must cultivate if you choose to remain as the demoted former CEO of your company. You must eat humble pie and swallow it with your pride every day. You must tell employees who commiserate with you about the good old days that the future with the new CEO will be better for them and the company. And then you must help that CEO execute on projects and plans that you personally may think are half-baked, dumb, impractical, or just plain crazy.

You might even have to help the new CEO implement a project or strategy this year that you rejected last year (when you were CEO) because you were certain it was doomed to fail. Maybe it was your resistance to this exact project or strategy that led to your downfall as CEO. Now you're expected to put your shoulder to the wheel and make it work.

Are you really up for that? Are you prepared to climb to the very top of The Founder Value Ladder? Are you ready to let go of the rungs you are clinging to? From my experience working with founders, almost all *think* they can accomplish this climb. But recalling the lessons of the Backwards Brain Bicycle, old habits are very hard to break, even if you believe you can. I've known only one founder who was really able to pull this off.

So be forewarned. When it's time to give up leadership of the company you founded, staying around to help out might feel like the easier path, but only because the pain of simply leaving might seem intolerable. To avoid the acute pain of cutting your ties to the company you founded, you prefer the low-grade chronic suffering of needing to bite your tongue, hiding your feelings, suppressing your ego, and working very hard at tasks you don't like, toward purposes you disagree with. Huh?

This is the price of staying. For the good of the company, if you stay, you must be prepared to support your successor without reservation.

"If you stay, you must be prepared to support your successor without reservation."

The transition from founder to new CEO is a fragile process that doesn't need interference from a meddling founder. Without a doubt, the new CEO will do things that will make it difficult for you to disguise your disgust. You will have to turn your back on long-time friends who come running to you for political support when the new CEO inevitably wants to replace them.

And some things at the company will go absolutely sideways. At that time, your job will still be to support your successor, the board's choice. To do anything less is to undermine your board. And then you invite dysfunction and chaos into the company that you raised, nurtured, and claim to love.

"You can't just ignore all the institutional memory and expertise I have."

I went through a long and expensive recruiting process with a venture-backed company as a candidate to replace the founder as CEO. The board had decided that change at the top was required, against the wishes of the founder. I interviewed with all of the board members and the founder, and I accepted the founder's explanation that although he was not in favor of being replaced, he would go along with his board, who controlled the decision anyway.

So imagine my surprise when, during my first day on the job, the clearly unhappy founder and former CEO called a company meeting without me present. Then, after calling me into the meeting already in progress, he introduced me like a puppy meeting my new family. I was a bit confused, because I thought I was hired to be the CEO and that he was now working for me. But the board never made it clear to the founder what his role would be and the limits on his newly restricted authority. By hiring the founder's replacement and not clearly delineating the changes in his authority, the board had set up both of us, and ultimately the company, for failure. I'm betting the board did not agree, but the founder thought he had a right to question and reject every initiative of mine with which he didn't agree. It certainly wasn't the way I envisioned my role.

Boards who force a founder transition, as well as founders who self-initiate this process, should first be completely clear about the founder's and new CEO's roles.

"Boards who force a founder transition, as well as founders who self-initiate this process, should first be completely clear about the founder's and new CEO's roles."

I'd strongly recommend that the successor take it upon herself to do everything she can to confirm this understanding, perhaps even in writing, before her first day. Without clear boundaries, it is way too easy for things to go awry. I've frequently come across this type of confusion of roles, even in situations where the founder voluntarily gave up the CEO role. In one such case, the founder expected to continue to represent the company during external corporate events. In another, the founder retained control over the financial books of the company and would not permit anyone else access to them, including the CEO.

To avoid situations like these, thoughtful companies with established CEO transition programs often prohibit the former CEO from having any continuing role at the company. As a matter of policy, they see there is more risk than reward in having a former CEO available for consultation or participating in a specific operating role. Former General Electric CEO Jack Welch famously gave up his operational role and his board seat at the time of his departure. Welch felt that not being around would enable his handpicked successor, Jeff Immelt, the best chance of success.

Transitions in CEOs are inevitable and necessary because people don't change at the same rate as the business environment.

"Transitions in CEOs are inevitable and necessary because people don't change at the same rate as the business environment."

CEOs who excel in one generation are unlikely to be a good fit for the next. Jack Welch built value at GE by reducing costs, cutting personnel, and making big acquisitions. This worked well in the economic environment of the 1980s and 1990s. The challenges Immelt has faced have been quite different in the 2000s. For instance, Immelt's strategy has been to embrace almost every aspect of sustainable "green" management, while Jack Welch never gave much more than lip service to global warming and other environmental issues, later admitting that it was only to be politically correct. Jeff Immelt had a very different set of challenges than did Welch, and it is unlikely that Welch would have flourished in this new environment.

TOUGHING IT OUT: HOW TO DEAL WITH THE NEW CEO IF YOU STAY

If you've chosen the tough road by staying with your company post-transition, then be prepared for the changes on their way, and accept the shift in authority that comes along with it. A founder with the right disposition, eager to see her organization succeed, can play an enormously important function by supporting and assisting her successor.

"A founder with the right disposition, eager to see her organization succeed, can play an enormously important function by supporting and assisting her successor."

Founders have insight into the products, technology, competition, and ins and outs of their teams. They can be great sounding boards for strategy and direction. But, as the saying goes, "If you are not part of the solution, you are part of the problem."

For the new CEO, the challenge is how to best tap into this font of founder knowledge without risking role confusion. One of the practices I found helpful as a successor was regularly scheduled one-on-one lunches between the founder and myself. These meetings enabled me to learn important lessons and gain insights from the founder. They served as a forum for testing out my new ideas, without any pretense of judgment or evaluation, and they were safe.

I often used these meetings for advice. As I reasoned earlier, asking for help from someone with wisdom is a sincere form of flattery. These meetings gave me a perspective that I could never gain on my own. And perhaps more important for me, it gave me a trusted friend with whom I could share many of the loneliest moments of being a CEO.

As a founder, you can be a valuable comrade to your successor. Most CEOs have no one else to turn to when they need to share their angst or when they are confronted by uncertainty. You can deliver a unique relationship that most CEOs don't have the good fortune of experiencing with anyone else.

In each of my six situations as a successor to the founder, there were important issues on which we disagreed. But if you are willing to step up, and realize that disagreements are inevitable even when trying to accomplish the same goals, your relationship with your successor can end up most successful. When a founder and I were able to have intelligent, unemotional discussions, we usually came to a mutually agreeable solution. Those situations reinforced our relationship and often led to positive outcomes for the company.

The only regretful outcome from these relationships is that on more than one occasion I succumbed to the founder's point of view, just to keep her happy. Often these compromises were personnel related—I agreed to keep people on board whom I should have replaced. It is difficult to execute change strategies without the right people in the right seats, but I let my relationship with the founder cloud my vision on some tough personnel changes.

ACCEPT CHANGES

Change at the top of most organizations usually comes too late. Investors with a stake in being regarded as founder-friendly will avoid replacing a founder until problems at the company have advanced much further than they should. Those who have experienced a founder transition process—including just about every venture capital firm—know it is too fragile to attempt unless absolutely necessary. Founders who initiate their own replacements follow a similar pattern. They will wait until they are completely convinced that they are not capable of reaching the next level, or they have failed on reaching a major milestone, before considering firing or demoting themselves.

So when the transition happens, the company is frequently in urgent need of change. To do this right, the founder who sticks around needs to accept and endorse the changes that the new CEO brings to the company.

"The founder who sticks around needs to accept and endorse the changes that the new CEO brings to the company."

When the venture-capital-controlled board suggested it was time to transition to a new CEO with a different skill set at Transcentive, as that successor I found many practices that had worked well to grow the company in its early days that would not work as we grew in scale.

Differentiating ourselves by customizing our software was perfect to help us navigate against our competition in the early days. However, continuing down this path would retard our future growth. Similarly, our sales team was also responsible for training our customers. This enabled our team to get funded sales trips while they were in the field training existing customers—a great strategy for saving money and enabling in-person sales calls on the cheap. However, we found that people who were great at training were not so good at the sales process and vice versa, so we ended up increasing our team's specialization and separating the teams.

Mike Brody's institutional knowledge was unsurpassed. It just so happens that much of what was now required to grow was outside his expertise and experience.

As a founder, it's really difficult to watch people change and mess with the things that you painstakingly erected to establish and support the business.

"As a founder, it's really difficult to watch people change and mess with the things that you painstakingly erected to establish and support the business."

Even transitions as scripted and carefully planned as that of GE are not completely smooth. Since his departure, Welch has publicly criticized Jeff Immelt for things that he has done differently than Welch would have preferred. Fortunate for Immelt and GE, by that time Jack no longer had any influence and was doing it from afar.

One founder I know well ran into a situation early in her transition. Her new CEO was about to make an obvious misstep in her handling of one of their most important strategic partners. But rather than stepping in to keep her from f**king up, the founder held back. Like a parent teaching a child how to ride a bicycle, she knew full well that she couldn't spend the rest of her time running along beside the new CEO's two-wheeler to keep her from falling off. Instead, she let her fall and trusted that she would learn an even more valuable lesson from the experience.

In my fourth gig, after my appointment as CEO the founder stuck around because he had a truly complementary skill set to mine. The company needed his skills and knowledge to be successful. He was one of the inventors of the technology and knew where the bodies were buried. He also had a significant stake in the success of the company. So his staying seemed to make sense to him and our board.

But he was far from happy being replaced. While I truly believe he liked me (at least during the recruiting process), in retrospect, it appeared that he agreed to hire me because I was his least offensive option. Not long after my hiring, he ended up conspiring with one of his colleagues, whom he had brought along from a former venture, to threaten to leave if the board didn't remove me. Knowing full well that the company couldn't survive at this early stage without at least one of these founders, I recommended the board relieve me of my duties, which they ultimately, but reluctantly, did. At least they did not reward his bad behavior by reinstalling him as CEO. Unfortunately, the die had been cast—the company skidded through the next few years and without ever returning the investors' capital.

If you've ever seen a bicycle built for two—a tandem—it's the perfect analogy for a founder who leaves her CEO role but decides to stick around. The rider at the front of a tandem is called the *captain,* and the one in back is the *stoker.* Only the captain steers the bicycle. That's the new CEO. In the back, the founder's role as the stoker is to contribute to the bicycle's forward thrust, in whatever direction the captain steers.

As a founder, if you decide to mount this tandem bicycle, you'd best be committed to not dragging your feet, shifting your weight, or doing anything that might cause the bike to crash, even if the direction you end up heading petrifies you.

You're the stoker, not the captain. Unless you want your organization to end up in a ditch, be the best stoker you can be, or just get off the bike.

"I started this company; I should still have some authority."

When you founded the company, one of your most important criteria for your early executives was loyalty. Now, if you've stuck around after a new CEO has begun, you are one of those executives. You will need to earn your new role with similar loyalty and remain an organizational lightning rod. Even the hint that you are not 100 percent convinced of your successor's authority will cause a highly charged current of dissent to surge within the organization.

One clear indication that your successor is not really in charge is if you retain your title and let your successor slide in alongside.

Co-CEOs, co-presidents, or even taking over the chairman role while your successor becomes CEO makes it clear who is still boss.

A year before they went public, Whole Foods hired Walter Robb. He first operated the Mill Valley, California, store and then rose through the ranks, becoming co-president in 2004 and then co-CEO, along with John Mackey, one of the two founders of the company. Robb oversaw six regions. Mackey and Robb have complementary skills and divided up responsibility for running the company between them. Although the structure lasted for a while, it remained unstable.

Whole Foods is a unique organization and seemed to have thrived under this management. But true to expectations, in November 2016 Whole Foods announced that it was transitioning from co-CEOs to a sole CEO with Mackey, its founder, taking back that role. Co-CEOs become popular when a founder brings in a senior executive to help propel the company to the next level but is not ready to give up the trappings of his office.

The only other time we hear of co-CEOs is when two companies merge and neither CEO wants to admit being vanquished. This too is an unstable state that only temporarily exists. According to Lindred Greer, who studies organizational behavior at the Stanford Graduate School of Business, multiple heads confuse teams and cause poor performance and conflicts among the leaders. Despite Whole Foods' anomalous but temporary success in maintaining co-CEOs, with one being a founder, this is a really difficult organizational structure to pull off.

Oracle went one step further. In September 2014, with great fanfare, Larry Ellison, founder and CEO, announced the appointment of co-CEOs to fill his shoes. They must be big shoes indeed to require both Mark Hurd, the former Hewlett-Packard CEO, and

Safra Catz, Oracle's longtime CFO, to fill them. Ellison demoted himself to chief technology officer. However, according to *Fortune*'s Adam Lashinsky, this rearrangement of management was largely for show. "The most shocking thing about the announcement is how little will change," Lashinsky said, alluding to the fact that it would be difficult for Ellison to give up his authority to anyone.

"When you have power, it becomes how you see yourself," said Greer. "Sharing that power with another is an unstable state of affairs."

ESTABLISH CLEAR AUTHORITY

As the founder, if you stay, you should publicly declare the new lines of authority in your relationship with the new CEO, as Ellison certainly did. Show up with your successor at a full company meeting and, in the most heartfelt manner possible, let your team know that you are transferring your authority to your new CEO and that you too will follow his lead. Ellison did this as well with his co-CEO team. After that, it's even more important to back up the public statement with actions. But even the most committed founder with an Academy Award–winning performance will be confronted by someone, often a long-term employee, trying to crack his façade.

When I took over for a longtime founder, a very capable woman who was running our East Coast sales team was unsure that she liked my style. That was probably an understatement. She sought out her friend and colleague, the founder, and expressed her concerns to him privately.

Despite his commitment to make our relationship work, the founder was caught in a bind.

Still present in the office nearly every day, he was an easy mark for his friend. With the best intention to avoid creating a rift between us, he listened attentively to her complaints, carefully avoiding expressing his opinion. Thinking that he had performed admirably, he told her he would communicate this to me, and came by my office for a chat.

He was startled when, after proudly reciting his tale of this discussion, I reacted negatively. I told him that his innocent action had set a negative tone for the organization. I suggested that word would get out that anyone who had a complaint about me had the ear of the founder. It didn't matter whether he agreed with the employee or not, but now all employees had a conduit for their grumbling.

We subsequently agreed that should an employee have any issue about the company that they raised with the founder, his response would be to accompany that employee to my office and have a three-way discussion as the very first step. Because most employees didn't really want to be called out for going behind my back, this divisive behavior stopped almost immediately. By withdrawing his willingness to even listen to gripes, we were able to positively impact the team's behavior.

As a follow-up, I initiated a discussion with the sales manager (the one who had already spilled her guts to the founder). While it didn't start out comfortably, we candidly talked through her issues. I dutifully thanked her for her honesty, setting the stage for a productive interaction. She went on to have a long and very successful career with the company, marrying one of our team members and creating a great family. She and I still joke about that conversation and how it ending up propelling us into a lifelong friendship.

The navigation of the founder-successor relationship is difficult from any angle. In my effort to maintain a cordial relationship with a particular founder, I mistakenly encouraged him to continue to preside at quarterly company meetings, even thought he was almost entirely absent from the company's day-to-day operations. Like the grandparent who on each visit spoils their grandchild, every meeting was like Christmas for our employees. These four-times-a-year festivities served to highlight the differences in our styles (his like Santa and mine like Scrooge), causing long-term employees to long for the past. Even with clarity of roles, this can be a tough navigation.

I joined Force 3 in 2008 to help out my friend Rocky Cintron, its founder, as the company began its next phase of challenges. Rocky had been at the helm of the company from its humble 8(a) beginnings (that's what our federal government calls a disadvantaged business) to a government-contracting powerhouse during the almost two decades from the time he founded the company. My job was to grow the company's value from there by improving profitability and increasing the value we delivered to our customers. To do this required changes in processes, systems, and people, the magnitude of which was not initially clear to either of us.

It was Rocky's intention that he would stick around. Having known Rocky for more than a decade, I figured we would have no issue working side by side. But almost from the start it became clear that my no-nonsense style of management by meritocracy clashed abruptly with Rocky's collegial style. With Rocky always nearby, anyone who didn't like what I had done would quickly consult him. Employee work that I rejected, Rocky praised. It was confusing to the employees. Several used our differences to their advantage. Others decided that if they could wear me out, they might get to return to Rocky—and the good old days. The safety net of a potential Rocky rebound staring them in the face neutralized almost anything that I intended to change.

If you remain nearby after giving up the CEO role, as Rocky

did, you offer an all-too-inviting alternative to your employees, your board, and your investors, should your successor stumble.

> *"If you remain nearby after giving up the CEO role . . . you offer an all-too-inviting alternative to your employees, your board, and your investors, should your successor stumble."*

While this may seem appealing as a hedge for your company's future, too often it becomes a self-fulfilling prophecy. It is hard to overcome the powerful relationship of a founder with his organization, even with the purposeful action of the founder. Anything short of complete exile will be viewed as a temporary condition.

Even when things are going well, there will always be staff members who long for the good old days when the founder presided. When Michael Bloomberg returned to his namesake company after his decade-plus-long sabbatical as mayor of New York City, his arrival in the office was enough to detract from the role and authority of his handpicked successor. "To the people in this company Mike is a God," stated Daniel Doctoroff, the CEO for the prior twelve years, as he abruptly voluntarily resigned to enable Bloomberg to retake the helm.

MOTIVATION REQUIRES COMMITMENT

Safety nets in general are a good idea. They can rescue and perhaps prevent the death of the high-wire walker should she stumble. But the one thing safety nets don't do is motivate.

Motivation requires commitment.

"Motivation requires commitment."

The ancient Greek warriors knew that commitment was a very powerful leadership weapon; this is why once their soldiers disembarked from their boats onto their enemy's shore, the Greek commanders would sound the order to "burn the boats!," giving their troops no alternative of retreat.

Founder transitions are tumultuous events. Most put the survival of your company and your financial future at stake. If the troops see the beloved founder as an alternative route for retreat, it will be difficult for your successor to ever motivate them to embrace and execute the difficult changes the company needs to grow and scale. Better you burn the boats!

"I don't like what they've done with the company."

After sixteen years of leading the company he founded, the CEO finally decided to relinquish the reins. He was certain he'd found the right successor. The two had worked together for most of the year, testing each other's personality and willingness to adapt to the other's quirks. "If we are not yet sure if we can work together, then we never will be," the founder told his soon-to-be successor.

It wasn't long after, though, that the founder grew wary of his new CEO. His successor decided that several of his earliest employees had no role in the new direction the company was to take. While he seemed to be treating these employees fairly by offering to buy out their restricted stock at the then-current value and to give them an extended notice period during which they could seek other employment, the founder grew concerned. His successor then began a strategic review of the sales process, reviewing pipelines and opportunities with a new level of scrutiny and accountability far different than the founder's style.

Then there was a drastic increase in the price of the software, followed by an incident with the new CEO offering to withdraw from a contract with one of the company's biggest customers. Then the new CEO announced a change in the company name. He renamed the baby, as if the baby were his own!

When the founder went home that night, he lamented to his wife that he felt it had been a mistake to hand off this company to his successor. He began to grow fearful that the mistake was compounding in impact every day he said and did nothing. He agonized over whether he should take action with his board and try to remove the new CEO before it was too late.

Instead, the founder decided that although changes were being made that he didn't particularly agree with, he would suspend his angst, at least for a while. He decided that instead of intervening and stopping what he didn't like, he would ask questions, add his thoughts, and provide his sage and experienced advice. But he never pulled rank, took over, or publicly expressed anything but his full and entire support for the new CEO. In company meetings, the CEO presided. During board meetings, despite the founder being designated as the chairman, the CEO ran the meetings. And when tough personnel decisions were made, the founder fell in line and let them happen, even when they impacted people with whom he had long-standing relationships.

After six years, sales at this company had quintupled from the day the new CEO had taken over. Some of the original employees were still around and had grown in responsibility and capabilities, as well as compensation. The founder and his successor had grown their friendship and their trust. They had figured out how to complement each other's styles and capabilities. The reward for his forbearance was a liquidity event from which the founder and several of the original employees realized a large payout—bigger than anything he had previously imagined.

While this situation worked out well, it was only due to the maturity and patience of this particular founder. Most situations where the founder remains do not end up this way. Unfortunately, too many times the estranged founder roots for his successor to be *wrong*.

"Unfortunately, too many times the estranged founder roots for his successor to be wrong."

Every disagreement is more fodder for plotting their successor's demise. It should be no surprise that a fissure at the top turns into a full-blown earthquake throughout the organization, often ending badly for both founder and successor.

Is it coincidental that in my set of experiences, the founders who accepted help were the recipients of sizable liquidity events? I'll leave that conclusion up to you.

ENCOURAGE CHANGE

If you remain on your board, as chairman or otherwise, remember that the reason there is a new CEO, the reason you were replaced, was to instigate change. Judging the new CEO against the yardstick of your former strategy is a surefire way to create friction and frustration for both of you. Remember the lessons you learned about how to best engage your board now with your new perspective as a board member.

Forbearance of this kind is easier if you have other things in your life besides your company. As soon after your transition as practical, take a long vacation. This time it does not have to be somewhere without cell service. Just delete the office speed-dial number from your phone. There is nothing that shouts transition louder than your lack of presence in the office. It gives your successor a chance to go it completely alone, even temporarily. But perhaps more importantly, it also gives you an opportunity to take some well-deserved time away without worrying about the company—worrying that isn't going to help anyway.

Many of the founders I have worked with now redirect their energies toward helping other founders with similar challenges to what they first encountered at their companies. There are those like Paul Thompson, who have taken on charitable work with similar zeal to his startup days. Others participate with investment funds, but most don't find participation with money quite as satisfying as the heat of the battle. Working as an advisor or sitting on the board of directors helps them satisfy their longing to be back in the hunt. But, most would admit, not completely.

Most of their risk-reward relationships have changed. No longer does a win at this level change their lives like what resulted from their founder roles. But money helps them keep score, and while they may not be risking everything (something I wouldn't recommend for any successful founder), they can generate leveraged wealth now with their investments rather than with their sweat. Responding to the request for help from fledgling entrepreneurs can provide a level of satisfaction that goes well beyond money. For the founder who desires to share his learning, there can be nothing more rewarding than mentoring a young founder and playing a role in their hard-earned success.

And what do you say?

What do you tell all the people you'll be leaving?

More importantly, what do you tell yourself?

I'm not retiring because I'm old or tired. I'm retiring because an organization has had twenty good years of me.

My success now will be determined by how well my successor grows the organization for the next twenty years. I've built a great management team, and they're ready to get me out of there so they can do their thing.

To be vital, an organization has to re-pot itself, start again, and seek new ideas. Renew itself.

I shouldn't stay on the board. I should disappear from the company so my successor feels totally free to do whatever he wants to do.

If I want to be back in the thick of things, I can go to another company to do that.

But here, I've done enough.

Those, in summary, are the words of Jack Welch when he left GE. Although he certainly wasn't the founder of GE, he understands the succession process as well as anyone. I couldn't have stated it any better. If this approach was good enough for Jack, I'm pretty sure it'll be good enough for you.

INDEX

S

Samaritan's Feet, 149
Sandlin, Destin, 34–35
"seagulling" behavior, 151–52
severance packages, 43, 103–5, 153
Shane, Mike, 123–24
skin-shedding process (molting), 86, 109
Sloan School at MIT, 2
Smarter Every Day (video series), 34
Smith School at Maryland, 2
Snider, Dee, 95
Stanford Graduate School of Business, 163
stress testing, 142
Strong, Vincent, 18
succession preparedness, 6, 133–50
  adjusting early to shift, 149–50
  building long runways, 136, 139
  charismatic founders, 139–41
  danger signs, 144
  delegating authority, 145
  demonstrating trust through behavior, 143–44
  emotional bond between founder and company, 135
  enlisting others as delegates of the mission, 134
  hiring planned successor, 136–37
  planning meetings without attending, 145
  rating key executives, 133–34
  relief from anxiety, 148
  removing concentration of risk, 146–49
  taking vacations, 146
  testing preparedness with temporary absences, 141–42, 145
  "try before you buy" concept, 137–39
superior knowledge or expertise
  to avoid questions, 78
  lack of advantage, 86–87

too much team camaraderie, 100–101
Suster, Mark, 74–75
Sywolski, Bob, 137–38

T

"talented terrors," 110–11
tandem bicycle analogy, 162
Tarpenning, Marc, 49
tasks, relinquishment of, 5, 45–65
  building institutional knowledge, 57–59
  detoxing customers' reliance on you, 55
  emotional attachment to personal importance, 53
  fear of offending customers, 52
  founder's responsibility, 59–60
  handing off deal-closing to sales staff, 62
  higher stakes have larger consequences, 63–65
  installing or upgrading CRM systems, 56
  letting others take over relationships, 45–47
  mandatory logging, 57–58
  regular proactive contacts, 58
  "rich or king" choice, 48–51
  rules for founders directly involved in deals, 61
  single point of failure, 53–55
  transitioning customer accounts to someone else, 52, 55
Tesla Motors, 49
"That customer and I have a long-standing relationship" cliché, 45–51
"That's how we do it here" cliché, 71–77
"That would mean giving up a key advantage" cliché, 83–88
"This company can't run without me" cliché, 146–50

ABOUT THE AUTHOR

 **LES TRACHTMAN** has spent the past two decades helping founders in half a dozen growing organizations and acting as a Sherpa for dozens of others. This book is the culmination of his years in the trenches and shares the lessons he learned from mentoring founders and from having hundreds of students at some of the country's leading business schools dissect his early cases. Trachtman's practical advice takes the topic out of the ivory tower into the bright light of reality.

Trachtman began his career as the fifth employee of a personal computer startup. Recruited by a classmate who graduated ahead of him, Les became infected with the entrepreneurial bug. Trachtman began to form the skills and mindset required to lead a technical startup.

After several stints as head of mergers and acquisitions for Hyperion Solutions and Progress Software, Trachtman was recruited to run his first venture begun out of the supercomputer lab at Yale University. It was here that Trachtman began his two decades of hands-on learning about what it takes to found and succeed a founder, some of which is documented in *Les is More Times Four*.

Trachtman served as Chief Executive Officer of this, his first startup—Metaserver—and then went on to work for and with founders at five other ventures including Force 3, a DC-beltway government contractor (sold to Sirius Computer Solutions); Transcentive, a pioneer in the employee stock option business (sold to Computershare); e-OneHundred Group, a compliance software company (sold to Stellent); and now—Purview, which focuses on disrupting the medical imaging business (where he purchased a controlling interest and works side by side with the founder). He also has served for the past twelve years as the only non-family member on the board of directors of The Metro Group, a ninety-year-old New York City–based services company.

Les Trachtman has taught and lectured at numerous universities including the Harvard Business School, the MIT Sloan School of Business, Rensselaer Polytechnic Institute, Kent State University, University of Maryland Smith School of Business, Union College, and Quinnipiac University School of Business. He frequently speaks at industry events including the Ernst & Young Entrepreneur of the Year Conference and has been the Entrepreneur in Residence at Union College, his alma mater. He writes the blog *Founder Transitions* (www.foundertransitions.com). Trachtman also has published articles in the *Harvard Business Review* and *Qunnipiac University Business*. A portion of his career is featured in the Harvard Business School case study *Les is More Times Four*, which educates entrepreneurs at leading business schools.

Trachtman grew up in New York and has lived in Atlanta, Boston, Connecticut, and Annapolis. He has traveled extensively across the globe and throughout the United States. He attended Union College where he received a BS in Electrical Engineering. He also attended Emory University, where he received his JD and MBA degrees.

Trachtman lives with his wife Michelle on the Severn River in Annapolis, Maryland, and has two grown children, Megan and Robbie.

Printed in Great Britain
by Amazon